DISPLACED PERSONS

Displaced Persons

Edited by

Kirsten Holst Petersen and Anna Rutherford

THE DOLPHIN No. 15

Acknowledgements

We wish to thank John Agard for his permission to print 'Listen Mr. Oxford don' which first appeared in *Mangoes and Bullets*, (Pluto Press). Claire Harris for her permission to reprint 'Policeman Cleared in Jaywalking Case', and Sam Selvon for permission to reprint extracts from *The Lonely Londoners*, (Longman). We also wish to thank Nikos Kypraios for his permission to use his painting 'The Stigma of Social Isolation,' for the cover of the book.

The cover illustration shows 'The Stigma of Social Isolation.' Painting by Nikos Kypraios.

Published by

SEKLOS
c/o Department of English
University of Aarhus
8000 Århus C DENMARK

General Editor: Anders Iversen

Production Editor: Connie N. Relsted

THE DOLPHIN - ISSN 0106-4487

Contents

Introduction

Kirsten Holst Petersen and Anna Rutherford

Peter Nobel's both concise and compassionate article 'Refugees and Other Migrants Viewed with the Legal Eye - or How to Fight Confusion' forms a natural introduction to the following texts. It describes the legal background and development of refugee definitions and the legal system set up to cope with refugees. Taking as his starting point the Universal Declaration of Human Rights (1948), Peter Nobel proceeds to discuss the Geneva Convention (1951), which he describes as Eurocentric and individual-orientated, for which reason it is mainly able to cope with individual, often well-educated and well-spoken dissidents. As Third World refugees often consist of large groups of peasants, uprooted because of a variety of destabilizing factors that do not come under the Geneva Convention, an important step in the development of International Law governing refugees was the OAU Convention (1974) according to which whole groups of people could gain refugee status. These are often referred to as 'de facto' refugees in the Western World, and they are the butt of restrictive legalization and persecution of governments in the rich Western part of the world, acting from motives of 'national egotism and self-rigteousness, cynical politics and ignorance.' Peter Nobel sees the 1980s as a period of 'rather nasty *Realpolitik* .' He puts this into perspective with some sobering figures. Of the estimated twelve to eighteen million refugees in the world 93% are taken care of in the already poverty-stricken Third World, and only 1% reaches Western Europe where they cause the present xenophobic and racist response. One of those responses is the concept of the economic refugee, purportedly just trying to enrich themselves at our expense. Through pointing out the political background to each of the refugee groups which have come to Western Europe within the last twenty years Peter Nobel argues pragmatically, but forcefully, against this point of view. The overall tenor of the article, however, is not pragmatic, but rather the expression of a deep concern for the plight of the refugee and the weakening of the moral and ethical fabric of the Western world in its dealing with the refugees. 'Things have changed in the 1980s,' he concludes, 'and not for the better.'

Salman Rushdie also takes a dim view of the present situation of refugees and migrants. His contribution was written during the race riots which swept through Tottenham and other inner cities in Britain in 1986, and he sees the violence and its causes in British society as the inescapable reality on which black and coloured writers in Britain must base their work. The emphasis is thus shifted away from strategies for coping with the situation, to the problems involved in literary representations of it. What sort of literature should a beleaguered racial, cultural and perhaps also linguistic minority write? Who should it write for? Salman Rushdie is well known for refusing to answer these questions, or to be prescriptive, and his answer here is in the same vein. He has adopted a strategy of 'eclecticism and mixtures,' and he suggests that this 'impurity' has in fact always been the norm rather than culturally 'pure" or unmixed forms. He does, however, point to some problems or dangers which face refugee or immigrant writers. The immigrant or refugee status places a responsibility on the writer to 'give voice' to his community. This can take two forms: one is to celebrate one's own people in stories and songs, but here Salman Rushdie sees a danger of glorifying the culture and creating stereotyped positive images instead of providing the community with 'fully realized human beings, as complex creatures, good and bad,' which Rushdie sees as the writer's true gift to his community. In connection with the problem of creating negative images of one's culture Rushdie discusses Hanif Kureishi's film *My Beautiful Laundrette,* and he defends the film-maker's right to criticize London's Asian community's 'fat cats.'

The other aspect of 'giving voice' is aimed at the dominant white culture and is therefore a public platform for the writer on behalf of his community. Here the writer becomes a representative for his community, and again this is something which Salman Rushdie categorically refuses to do whilst often doing it anyway, maybe not directly in his creative writing, but certainly in his polemic writing. He thus not only discusses, but also exemplifies the dilemma which faces the writer from a refugee or immigrant community.

In the next article Sneja Gunew explores those difficulties in a specific context - that of Australian migrant writing. In one sense all Australians, except the Aboriginals are immigrants, but in present-day Australia a distinction is made between Anglo-Celtic immigrants and others who are called 'ethnics.' These others have the status of immigrants or refugees, and although they form a significant part of Australia's population they are still marginalised vis-a-vis the Anglo-Celtic majority who hold the economic and political power. While white immigrants, other than the English have always been present throughout the history of Australia the main influx came as a result of a political decision and the establishment of the Australian Department of Immigration in 1945. The reason was a need for manpower to man the construction projects and industries of post-war Australia. The main target group was still the English, but the need was so great that Australia signed migration agreements with a number of European countries, and Greece and Italy quickly became the sources of immigration. Italian is the second language after English in Australia, and Melbourne is the third largest Greek speaking city in the world after Athens and Thessaloniki.

Another major group consisted of displaced persons, mainly Eastern Europeans who had been uprooted by World War II. Amongst those the most significant single group is the Poles of whom there are more than 125.000 in Australia. It will be obvious that all these groups are white, and until into the 1960s Australia had a 'white immigrants only' policy. This has changed now, giving way to immigrant

groups from South East Asia and refugee groups from Chile, Lebanon and most recently, from Sri Lanka, Ethiopia and Vietnam (the boat people). The immigrants quickly became absorbed into the expanding industry, and as industrial workers they did not always lead enviable lives. Peter Lyssiotis' imaginative photomontages are an eloquent and moving statement about those conditions, aptly expressed by the text on one of his photo-montages 'to those lands which have machines workers shall be given.'

Sneja Gunew also takes a strong position by asserting that migrant writing offers new possibilities. not already covered by the literature of the dominant culture. One of the main obstacles is the language, not to master it, but how to make it an authentic vehicle for experiences and a consciousness which was formed in another language and by another culture. It is important, Sneja Gunew maintains, that the migrants are left to speak for themselves, to fashion their new world themselves. In the resulting body of writing a pattern is discernible. The first wave tends to be nostalgic about the old world, but this mode is rejected by the next generation who have absorbed aspects of 'mainstream' culture and thus live in a world of mixed values. This world of crossroads is seen as a vital possibility for renewal and change, as it is forced into recognizing the relativity - and hence the mutability - of social customs and values. Ideally, in a multicultural society there should not be a mainstream versus peripheral cultures, but a series of different, but equal cultures, all enriching their common country by their diversity. This is, however, not the case in Australia, where the mainstream culture is firmly 'male Anglo-Celtic,' and migrant writing tends to relate in some way (usually antagonistically) to this. As an example of migrant writing which forms a maximum contrast both in form and content to mainstream expectations and stereotyping Sneja Gunew discusses two experimental migrant women poets. To explain the distance between the poetry of Ania Walwicz (Polish) and Antigone Kefala (Romanian, Greek) and male Anglo-Celtic expectations of migrant women Sneja Gunew starts the discussion by outlining the roles allotted to migrant women in mainstream writing in which they signify 'excessive sexuality, food, factory-fodder, and silence.' If they break their silence they are expected to do so in broken English and only to tell the story of their uprooting and difficulties in the new world. If these stories belong to literature at all, they belong to the oral tradition, but mainstream critics see them as belonging primarily to the areas of sociology or history, and as such they need to be interpreted by competent researchers to yield up their full meaning. If any of these stories show signs of being other than 'unmediated confessions,' for example through the conscious use of crafted language, this is usually ignored. To choose to discuss poetry, which is the form demanding the highest linguistic skill, written by migrant women, who are considered the most silent and unsophisticated group, is thus tantamount to an aggression, and by pointing out in her analysis of the two poets the careful and conscious use of language to transform the migrant experience into an artistic statement Sneja Gunew makes a convincing case for her argument, which is that writing by migrant women in Australia is a valuable addition to mainstream writing and that it contains possibilities for renewal, which are not present in the male Anglo-Celtic tradition.

Rada Usak - Yugoslavia migrant meat factory worker. Photo: Vivienne Mehes.

The reader can test these assertions for herself by reading the contributions by migrant writers. In her piece 'Towards a Language' Antigone Kefala tells her story of migration from Romania to Greece to New Zealand to Australia. However, her emphasis is on the linguistic odyssey, through Romanian, Greek, and English. Asserting that 'the basic assumptions of a language come out of a way of life, a past history, cultural and moral norms,' she explores what happens to both language and experience when this connection is severed.

From across the world the Dutch Canadian writer Aritha van Herk throws light on Antigone Kefala's problem in her contribution 'Placing Truth or Fiction.' 'It is language, after all, that accomplishes displacement,' she says. 'Emotion and idea have some influence but without language they do not exist.' When she realizes that she knows Dutch without being aware of it, she also knows, that she can never be pure, and that 'the only verities are words, language.' This realization turns her into a writer of fiction, which in this view is the only truth.

Ania Walwicz continues the exploration of language. In a short statement she says that she is interested in experimental writing, 'in the sound information of language and in capturing the immediacy of experience through language.' This is exemplified by her amazing prose poems which rely on verbal images and imaginative associations to create crystal clear states of feeling of loneliness, unbelonging, and fear.

The short story 'What is in the name?' manages to be amusing about a very serious aspect of migrant problems: the way the host culture fails to cope with their different sounding names, and by extension, cultures. Zeny Giles (Greek) continues the section of fiction by Australian migrant women with a short story 'The Questioning of Persephone MacDougall' which explores the loneliness of a cross-cultural position, which entails partial loss of the old and only partial participation in the new, and it also gives an insight into the difficulties of growing old in a migrant situation. Being young in a similar situation is evidently not easy either, and in 'White Sex' Vilma Sirianni (Italian) explores the difficulties of receiving a strict Italian sexual upbringing in Australia.

With 'Making Connections' Chitra Fernando moves the centre of attention away from the European migrants and on to a Sri Lankan family. Here one feels that the cultural gap has widened, and that the main character, the man of the family is not only alienated from his wife and daughters who have taken to modern living, but also from his dreams and aspirations, and he pulls himself out of his despair through a very Indian and non-Western epiphany which urges him to see connections between things in this new and alien world.

Another wave of post World War II emigrants went to England from the colonies, particularly the West Indies. The reasons were the same: dismal conditions in the home country combined with a British need for a workforce, but the circumstances were different. The West Indian emigrants were indoctrinated with British values through their education, they held British passports and felt a sense of belonging, even homecoming as loyal subjects of the Queen. As happened to the immigrants in Australia they got the dirtiest, hardest and lowest paid jobs, and they encountered racism which took many of them by surprise. Sam Selvon left Trinidad in 1950 armed with a romantic vision of the English landscape, which he got from reading Wordsworth, and an idealized view of the English, who, however, deceived him. In London he was thrown in among other West Indians and here he discovered his fellow countrymen, and it is they who form the subjects of his fictions. He also had to grapple with the language, and not until he stopped trying to write received English and found his own style, using aspects of West Indian English, did he succeed in creating his marvellous world of black Londoners. The outstanding feature of his humour is a monument to West Indian resilience, as the topic is depressing: loneliness, poverty and racism are the objective conditions of Selvon's lonely Londoners, but a sense of community rather than despair or bitterness is the overwhelming feeling of the book, and this is seen to conquer the difficulties of the hostile environment.

The writers who formed the second wave of immigrants from the West Indies to England have lost some of the patience, and anger rather than humour is the basic tone of their writing. David Dabydeen came to England in 1969 and went through the classic motions of a promising, but poor young writer: poverty, homelessness, state care, and finally Cambridge on a scholarship. He is more sure of himself than the earlier writers. Linguistically, this shows itself in his confident use of Guyanese English. The language itself makes a statement about the relativity of value systems by ignoring conventional grammar and creating a strong and unique voice, which is evidently better suited to the Caribbean experience than conventional English. This sense of liberation from the obligation to write gramatically correct British English is expressed in the poem 'Listen Mr. Oxford don' by one of David Dabydeen's contemporaries, John Agard. The poem may be funny and light-hearted, but the many layers of meaning in lines like 'I slashing suffix in self-defence/ I bashing future with present tense' is a good example of the interdependence of linguistic and mental independence. In a more serious vein David Dabydeen's poems exhibit this liberation from the strictures of English education. His poems show great courage in touching the raw nerves of pain, both in the home experience of slavery and poverty and in the exile experience of betrayal.

Another member of the group of radical young West Indian writers, loosely based in London, is Caryl Phillips, and he shares Peter Nobel's view of a deepening crisis in race relationships. In the 50s, when the first wave of immigrants arrived there was first curiosity, then hostility. Today he thinks 'it's almost hostility distilled.' This inevitably brings in the subject of repatriation, but Caryl Phillips feels that it is not possible to go back, rather one must struggle to be accepted. Caryl Phillips writes about both his Caribbean as well as his English experience, because to write only about the English experience would turn him into a protest writer: rage would become his main theme, and this would stifle him as a creative writer. Like Salman Rushdie he refuses to become a spokesman for his group, and yet in his writing this is often exactly what he becomes. He does, however, also face the problem which Salman Rushdie raised in connection with Hanif Kureishi, that of being considered a traitor if he criticizes aspects of his West Indian community. Caryl Phillips is extraordinarily sensitive to the rough deal metered out to women by West Indian men, and in his novel *The Final Passage* he brings to the surface the women's pain in a way not unsimilar to Alice Walker's in

The Color Purple . The problems of allegiance and spokesmanship still dog the writers.

Like the women migrant writers in Australia the West Indian woman writer Claire Harris chooses not only to represent, but to identify with her subject, a juvenile black girl, arrested and stripsearched for jaywalking. By identifying with the girl she makes the (unpunished) crime against her a crime against all black women. She resembles David Dabydeen in her courage to deal with an extremely painful subject matter, and the prose poem seems to be a form well suited to recreating 'inner states of emotion,' as Ania Walwicz did.

'Inner states of emotion' are also the subject of the contribution by the well-known Pakistani actor Zia Mohyeddin. He initially came to England in search of drama and therefore considered himself a migrant. Like writers, actors also work with language and are forced to take a stand, and Zia Mohyeddin rejected the accent, which he calls the 'Peter Seller's accent,' and which he was supposed to talk on account of his brown skin, and vowed to speak only pure English. Despite his success this rejection of his background nagged at him, and eventually he felt compelled to return to Pakistan, only to be censured and forced to return to England, this time as an exile. He finds the state of exile very different from that of being a migrant in that it precludes the possibility of return, and this forces him to engage more seriously with the host country, and at the same time it brings about a certain nostalgia for roots. Zia Mohyeddin solves the contradictions by extolling the tolerance and accommodation of the British democratic tradition and at the same time doing readings and recordings of both prose and poetry in Urdu.

This volume is produced and published in Denmark, and this should be reflected in the book. The interview with people from the 1001 Night restaurant joins the rest of the contributions in its catalogue of difficulties, faced by migrants and refugees, and in addition it offers a view of Danes as seen from the outside, and this is a perspective which offers yet another angle from which migrant views and writing can enrich the host country and help break down monolithic notions of cultural purity.

Aarhus University, Denmark. Photo: Poul Lind-Petersen.

Refugees and other Migrants Viewed with the Legal Eye - or How to Fight Confusion

Peter Nobel

The Confusion

The man in the street in Islamabad, Khartoum or Mexico City must be rather confused over the refugee problem. The same can be said about the reader of *The Daily Telegraph* in London, *Le Figaro* in Lyon or *Dagens Nyheter* in any Swedish town. If he or she is not an expert in contemporary migration patterns or refugee law it is hardly possible to find a clear way through the mist of unexplained and often misunderstood words and expressions: refugees, uprooted, displaced persons, asylum seekers in a refugee-like position, economic migrants, *de facto -* refugees etc., words and expressions which are often misunderstood by journalists as well. The humanitarian mind is hoping for assistance and protection for everyone in need of it. Racists, extreme nationalists and xenophobics write, paint and scream: "Stop the immigrants!" Politicians and the mass media show a tendency to fool each other into believing that things are worse than they are. In the meantime the decent citizen, whether in the rich western countries or the poor countries of the Third World think that those in need must be helped by their fellow human beings. The citizens endowed with this kind of decency seem to be clearly more numerous in Africa than in North West Europe or in the USA. But even humanitarianism and solidarity come under strain when exposed to confusion and uncertainty as to whom should be entitled to protection and assistance and who should not.

This lack of knowledge, understanding and guidance is found to a varying degree in most countries in the world. It is found among the public, the politicians, the decision makers as well as amongst those who have to execute orders and implement rules and laws. The first sufferer is the newly arrived alien who is victimized and suffers from the ignorance of those who hold power over his destiny, and his deep feeling of insecurity is both painful and traumatizing.

The Importance of Law

Migration and its components are not seen and described in the same way by sociologists, antropologists, psychologists or lawyers. I maintain that the legal aspect is very important. It is the law that decides what status shall be given to a person by the State on whose territory or under whose jurisdiction he finds himself. (I am not happy with the modern concept of statehood, but that is another matter). It is the law that makes it clear to that State and the international community what their obligations and powers are in relation to that person. It is the law, that provides the categorization making it clear to each of the international organizations, who is under its mandate and responsibility and who is not.

The history of refugee law and the concept of asylum goes back beyond the written history of mankind. With a new start between the two world wars international refugee law has developed within the framework of the international code of Human Rights. What has happened in the decades after the Second World War is of particular significance. It is the result of the patient work of good hearts and clear minds often faced with opposition from national egoism and self-rightousness, cynical politics and - again - ignorance. The progress made should be honoured as the civilizational achievement wihch it is. Above all, the principles enshrined in all these international legal instruments related to refugees and human rights should be held in respect and implemented. If they were, a great deal of suffering and seemingly hopeless problems would disappear. We are, in the late 1980-s obviously going through a rather nasty period of *Realpolitik* . Still it is very much a question of disseminating the rules as a first step towards their recognition and implementation. A description of the legal system for the protection of refugees indirectly, though unmistakeably, shows what is missing in the system: There is still gross violation of human rights for which there is seemingly no remedy and there is the category of sufferers who fall outside the system and for whom there is no protection or assistance, not even on paper.

In the following pages I intend therefore to give a brief presentation on how refugee law and refugee situations have developed in the last forty years since the Second World War. This will also give me an opportunity to touch upon neighbouring categories of migrants and related issues.

Starting with the definition of a refugee as contained in the 1951 Geneva Convention I will then examine the complimentary provisions in regional and legal instruments.

International Refugee Law and Machinery under the auspices of the UN

The governments and peoples who rose out of the wreckage of the Second World War formed the new universal body, the United Nations, with the overruling sentiment "Never more". Never more should warmongers and fascists be allowed to impose such disasters upon mankind, never more should such racist genocide occur, never more should torture, forced labour, arbitrary deprivation of freedom and all other atrocities be possible. With all this in mind the young UN conceived and adopted the *Universal Declaration of Human Rights of 10 December 1948* .

Let us look briefly at just one half of its thirty articles, art. 14.1:

> Everyone has the right to seek and to enjoy in other countries asylum from persecution.

This is in order to make three points. First, that refugee law is an inseparable part of the code of Human Rights. Second, everyone without exception has the right to flee and to seek asylum so long as the cause for the flight is persecution. Third, governments or their branches or other agencies are acting contrary to the universal principles of Human Rights when they create obstacles making it increasingly difficult for asylum seekers to move between countries or to leave their own, if they are threatened.

The Universal Declaration is as it says just that - a declaration - which means, it is not like a legally binding treaty. The pressure that can eventually be exercised against an erring government, if any, is therefore more of a political or moral character. The Declaration indicates the direction and the outlines which the states are supposed to follow when developing in detail international legal instruments and domestic legislations designed to meet the requirements of the Declaration. The years immediately after its adoption saw much diligent work and hope-inspiring progress in many fields, of which the *European Convention for the Protection of Human Rights and Fundamental Freedoms 1950* and the *Convention relating to the Status of Refugees, adopted in Geneva in 1951,* are good examples. The definition of a refugee as contained in the 1951 Geneva Convention relating to the Status of Refugees (189 UNTS 137), which in this paper is referred to as the Geneva Convention, is often said to be eurocentric and outdated. I would agree with this but I also have to agree with those who find it totally unrealistic to expect for the time being that international consensus could be reached on amendments to the Geneva Convention. Therefore we are bound to continue our support and try to promote other developments. The Geneva Convention is the universal basic definition which can pragmatically be expanded, when need arises by extending the mandate of the UN High Commissioner for Refugees (UNHCR) through resolutions by the UN General Assembly and by the adoption of regional instruments complementary to the universally respected Geneva Convention.

The central part of the Geneva Convention's definition says:

> ...the term "refugee" shall apply to any person who...owing to well-founded fear of being persecuted for reasons of race, religion, nationality, membership of a particular social group or political opinion, is outside the country of his nationality and is unable or, owing to such fear, is unwilling to avail himself of the protection of that country; or who, not having a nationality and being outside the country of his former habitual residence as a result of such fear, is unwilling to return to it.

From the beginning the Geneva Convention was limited to events in Europe which had occurred before 1st January 1951. With the adoption in New York of the

1967 Protocol Relating to the Status of Refugees (606 UNTS 267) a possibility was made available to abolish both the geographical and time limit. Most of the states have made use of this opportunity. It was with the 1967 Protocol that the Geneva Convention became the universal instrument of refugee law. The Convention has been ratified by approximately one hundred states and enjoys its strongest support in Western Europe, Latin America and Africa. The USA, which has signed the Protocol but not the Convention, nevertheless, in principle, respects the latter. Finland has ratified it and so has Yugoslavia. On the other hand, no country in the Eastern block has aceeded to it. In the Middle East the only signatories have been Iran and Israel. In the Far East progress of refugee law has been slow but since 1980 the important ratifications of Japan, the Peoples' Republic of China and of the Phillipines have been made. Even many states, which have not so far aceeded to the Geneva Convention, generally respect the principles enshrined therein. These have therefore taken on the dignity of international customary law in territories which are not directly bound by them, as they are by treaty law. This in turn is an important aspect when considering refugee determination.

Many developing countries have hesitated to become contracting parties to the Geneva convention, not because they are not willing to receive and protect asylum seekers, but because of the far-reaching rights and favours it accords to refugees, favours that these countries cannot always grant their own nationals - for instance education or social security. In other cases certain Third World countries have had a very negative attitude towards admitting refugees into their own territory.

Let us turn back to the refugee definition in the Geneva Convention. This classical definition is based on the concept of "well-founded fear", which seems to be an objective criterion until one realises, that a certain fear may be less well-founded in one individual than in another, which in turn brings us back to the subjectivity of the asylum seekers. This approach is very much focussed upon the individual, even if the reasons of race, religion etc. can open a way to more collective refugee recognition of a *prima facie* character. Persecution is not defined in the Geneva Convention. It is supposed to define itself, albeit in a circular way. Persecution is at hand when it is of a nature to inspire well-founded fear and the fear is well-founded, when it is caused by the danger of persecution. When this definition was drafted almost forty years ago the authors probably had less difficulties with the interpretation and the application of this text, than we do today. What they had in mind was the European experience from the Second World War and the refugee situation in Europe at that time. The eurocentricism of the Geneva Convention therefore was not only tied to the geographical limitation prevailing before the 1967 Protocol. It lies imbedded in the very construction of the Convention itself, not least in the refugee definition.

Persecution can be understood in terms of denial of basic Human Rights. If a person in the country where he is living risks being subjected to torture or to cruel, inhuman or degrading treatment or punishment, of if he can be arbitrarily arrested or detained there, it is obvious that he is in danger of being persecuted in the sense of the Convention.

The world was soon forced to realise that people were compelled to leave their home countries and seek safety elsewhere for many other reasons than the fear of individual persecution based on race or political opinion or any of the other three classical causes. Armed conflicts of one kind or another, serious disturbances of public order and many other sorts of pressure and oppression can make life so dangerous and unbearable that people are unable to stand it and they have to flee to save themselves. Such safety-seekers who were refugees but who were not covered by the Geneva Convention, became the centre of much debate, often under the name *de facto* refugees. Most of them originated in Third World countries and most of them have also found refuge in such countries. They are a typical Third World phenomenon. After much hesitation and discussion these so-called *de facto* refugees came to be recognized as such in most First World countries, either by direct legislation granting them asylum or by generous practice in issuing residence permits. They are also referred to as B-refugees, safety-seekers in a refugee-like situation.

The expression "basic" Human Rights has been used in reference as a means for establishing what shall be considered as persecution under the Geneva Convention. The Human Rights law has undergone a rapid and extensive development. Scholars now refer to first generation rights, second generation rights and also rights of the third generation. What is a "basic right" is a question that is met with different answers from time to time and from place to place. Not to be subjected to torture is a basic human right everywhere. Where torture occurs it is one of the most serious violations of the international law of Human Rights. But if someone is denied education in a country which has not yet been able to build up an educational system, it does not of course constitute a breach of the law. On the other hand, if someone is discriminated against and refused entrance to school because he belongs to a minority, then it is a different matter, as the principle of non-discrimination is one of the most important and most often repeated in a number of international Human Rights instruments. Such discrimination can eventually, in combination with other circumstances, constitute persecution.

Another major step forward in the development of International Refugee Law was the OAU Convention Governing Specific Aspects of Refugee Problems which was adopted in Addis Ababa in 1969 and came into force in 1974. Whereas the Geneva Convention was Eurocentric, based on the European war experience, the OAU Convention was Africa-centred, based on the assumption that most African refugees had originated in countries still under colonial or white minority regimes, and this was reflected in the Convention.

It was within this instrument that the most important step was taken in international law to expand the refugee definition from the euro-centric and individual-oriented one of the Geneva Convention into a concept that could correspond to the demands of the massive groups of safety-seekers in the Third World and the causes of their fears.

The positive elements, the inclusion clauses, of this African refugee definition are presented in two parts. The first simply repeats the well-known definition of the Geneva Convention with its "well-founded fear" of being persecuted for any of the five classical reasons of race, religion etc.

The second part is quoted *in extenso* :

The term "refugee" shall also apply to every person who, owing to external aggression, occupation, foreign domination or events seriously disturbing public order in either part or the whole of his country of origin or nationality, is compelled to leave his place of habitual residence in order to seek refuge in another place outside his country of origin or nationality. (Art. 1.2.)

This part does not speak of the subjective fear of the individual but of objective criteria: unbearable and dangerous conditions which cause entire populations to flee. This is the legal basis for admitting refugee masses upon a group determination of their status. The wording "events seriously disturbing public order" should adequately cover a variety of man-made conditions which prevent humans from residing safely in their countries of origin, as well as natural disasters if they are aggravated by violence or political action or neglect. The African definition solved many of the problems, which have so often been discussed under the term "de facto" refugees, by including among the refugee-generating factors the warlike or suppressing events or serious disturbances of public order which are tragically common in the world today. It also avoided other difficulties sometimes encountered under the Geneva Convention's definition, when the refugee-generating conditions are only found to prevail in a part of the country of origin. The African definition therefore has had an impact on many parts of the world outside of Africa. For refugee definition in the Third World it is the obvious platform. After the Conference on the Situation of Refugees in Africa held in Arusha in Tanzania in 1979 this definition was cemented and there are reasons to believe that the refugees of Africa have benefitted from the OAU Refugee Convention, but it has not diminished their numbers. In the ten years after its adoption the refugees in the continent were redoubled several times over resulting in estimates in 1979 of more than four million refugees in Africa. This time only about one-fourth of them were assumed to have originated in white minority-ruled countries and consequently around three million in OAU member states. Since this estimate was made the differences in these proportions have become even greater as most Zimbabwean refugees could return in early 1980 following the independence of their country while the total numbers of refugees in Africa continued to grow in the 1980s. In 1977 a specialist described the situation like this:

...it is known that refugess in Africa belong,
generally speaking, to two categories:
- massive, very often numerically important
refugee groups of rural origin, and
- scattered individual refugees or refugee
families living in urban areas.

The conference also recommended (in Rec. 7.5.) that the United Nations should apply the 1979 OAU Refugee Convention including, of course, its refugee definition. The General Assembly of the UN finally in a particular resolution in November 1979 fully endorsed all the recommendations of the Arusha Conference. With this the African refugee definition of the OAU Convention has gained universal recognition both legally and politically.

Those who are excluded from refugee status and those who have ceased to be refugees.

We have dwelt upon the most important positive elements in the unversal criteria for refugee determination. They tell us who shall be included in the refugee definition and be accorded refugee status. Such rules are called *inclusion-clauses*. But there are circumstances, which can exclude a person from refugee status although he might otherwise qualify and be eligible. They are regulated in *exclusion-clauses*. Finally the conditions which once turned someone into a *bona fide* refugee by definition, might have changed and ceased to exist so there is no longer ground for the former refugee to enjoy refugee status and rights. Therefore there are also *cessation-clauses*. We shall have a brief look into the exclusion- and cessation-clauses in the Geneva Convention.

The exclusion-clause in the Geneva Convention names three categories of persons to whom the provisions of the Convention does not apply. The first group are those who receive - or who are supposed to receive one is tempted to say - protection or assistance from organs of the UN other than UNHCR. Today the only category of this kind is the Palestinian refugees in the Near East, who ought to be assisted by the UN Relief and Works Agency for Palestine Refugees in the Near East (UNRWA).

The second category in the exclusion clause are such persons who, by the competent authorities in their country of residence, are recognized as having the rights and obligations of nationals.

The third category is reserved for certain malefactors. Thus the Convention shall not apply to any person with respect to whom there is serious reason to believe that he has committed a crime against peace, a war crime, a crime against humanity, a serious non-political crime outside the country of refuge and prior to his admission to that country or, finally, acts contrary to the purposes and principles of the UN. A refugee who commits a crime in the country of asylum shall be punished according to the law of that country following a conviction reached through due legal process.

The cessation-clause lists the following circumstances under which the Convention should cease to apply to a person; if he has voluntarily re-availed himself of the protection of his country of nationality or re-acquired such nationality; if he enjoys the protection of the country of his new nationality; if the circumstances in connection with which he was first recognized as a refugee have ceased to exist. These are the most important items on that list.

Refugees and other Migrants in the rich Countries of the West.

We have dealt with the emergence of international refugee law as a part of the International Code of Human Rights. It has become evident that the legal concept of refugees has widened to include categories of safety-seeking migrants who are not included in the refugee-definition of the Geneva Convention. In the poor countries of Africa, Asia and Latin America there is no reason for and therefore no administrative machinery for individual refugee determination nor for distinguishing between refugees, so-called economic migrants, or people uprooted because of natural catastrophies. By and large the debate and the scrutiny in individual cases is typically found in the rich countries in North-West Europe and in the USA. But before entering into this subject a few remarks should be made about *demography* and *refugee-statistics* .

It is important to understand that there are no reliable figures for the international movements of refugees and other migrants. We have to work with some kind of estimates and I would suggest that in mid-1987 there were between twelve and eighteen million refugees in the world. Somewhere near half of them originate from two countries, Afganistan and Ethiopia. The majority are found in the Far, Middle and Near East, in Africa and in Central America. Few of them are found outside these regions. Most of them live near the only international border they have ever crossed or *will* ever cross. Their hope is to return just like tens of millions before them in contemporary history have returned to India, Pakistan, Bangladesh, Algeria, Angola, Zimbabwe, Greece, Spain, Portugal, Argentina and Uruguay - to give just a few examples - after independence or democracy have been gained or conditions in these countries have improved. Most of these peoples have rural backgrounds, literacy is low and few of them tend to move from the camps where they have settled.

A few however have education, relatives, contacts, money, influence, wit and will or just restlessnes enough to proceed to the rich countries. It is estimated that about 3 percent of the entire refugee population in the world arrives annually in the rich countries, 1 percent to Western Europe, and the rest to the USA, Canada and some to Australia. It was said that during 1986 there were between 140.000 and 200.000 new asylum seekers in Western Europe, a figure which supports the estimates made earlier.

At the same time in 1986, according to The Council of Europe sources the total immigration to Western Europe was around two million. Yet all the discussion and all the controversy seems to be focused on the asylum seekers. The fact that the majority of them these days come from non-European countries has in many places infected the debate with the venomous taste of racism. Things have changed in the 1980s and not for the better.

During the decades of reconstruction in Europe after the Second World War, foreign labour was needed, welcomed and sometimes actively recruited to Western Europe. Not everything that was done was wise or morally acceptable. Take for example the French system, found also in other countries. The illegal immigrants, *les clandestins*, were tolerated as long as they did not go into politics or create problems of any kind. Such people lived for years without any legal status or corresponding security, thrown to the mercy of unscrupulous employers and landlords who were more than ready to exploit them and then reject them when their labour was no longer needed. The German-Austrian *Gastarbeiter* system also bred inequality, injustice and discrimination; whilst the neglect of the British Tory Government towards immigrants and ethnic minorities many formerly subjects of its Empire, has created an explosive and dangerous situation of fear and despair. Yet during the boom years of the 1960s and 1970s the Western World in its quest for labour was open for immigration and these countries were considered the best allies of the UN High Commissioner for Refugees and his efforts to resettle refugees. Before turning to the much more serious aspect of 1987 we will have a short look at the legal solutions found in these countries.

All the states of Western Europe including Finland and Turkey have ratified the Geneva Convention. They have also acceded to the 1967 Protocol, though Italy and Turkey have so far maintained the geographical limitation of the Geneva Convention with the result that neither of these countries can accord the legal status of refugee to anyone from outside Europe.

Until the beginning of the 1980s the refugee definition of the Convention was mostly given a rather wide interpretation. But the appearance of new categories of safety-seekers who could not be placed under that definition, generated a debate full of obscurity and misunderstanding. The fact that most of these asylum-seekers arrived from other regions: the Middle East, Asia, Africa and Latin America has sharpened the differences and has aggravated and made it more difficult to take correct soundings of the events. A clear line of demarkation has been visible between those antagonistic towards this new wave of immigration and those moved by humanitarian feelings. It has not been uncommon to see governments and authorities being bitterly criticized by some of the best people in the voluntary agencies.

It has often and with emphasis been propounded from some quarters that a large portion of those coming from the Third World in particular, are not "real" or "political" refugees. They should be considered instead to be "economic refugees" or luck-seekers, "economic migrants" just hoping for a better life. It is not surprising that the people from the poor countries on the Earth find their way to the rich ones, especially as the latter give no evidence of any real good will towards a just and fair global distribution of goods, resources, assets or burden. Such migration must be expected and may to some extent already be taking place. Legally, politically and morally one should be prepared for such a future and preferably with less primitive and more humane methods than the heavily guarded frontiers of today with immigration control ultimately depending on force and violence and contempt for other peoples. But there is not one example in contemporary history of any catastrope in the Third World: draught, famine, flood or earthquake, which has generated any notable increase in Third World immigration to the rich countries. On the contrary any such notable increase has been directly referable to a political event. From the Western European horizon it is easy to give examples: the Hungarian revolt in 1956, the Military Junta in Greece in 1967, the coup in Prague in 1968, Allendes overthrow in Chile in 1972, the Islamic Revolution in Iran and the following attack from Irak in 1980, military take-overs in Turkey and Poland 1981 and the Tamil conflict in Sri Lanka in 1985. The list could be made much longer. To it should be added political situations like those in the Lebanon, Eritrea, Uganda, Bangladesh and Central America which are of long duration rising at intervals to crisis points. Chileans did not arrive before 1972, Lebanese not before 1975, when the internal war started. Very few

To those LANDS which have MACHINES WORKERS SHALL be GIVEN

Photo: Peter Lyssiotis.

Iranians came before 1980 although there were a few refugees from the harsh rule of the Shah. Most Eritreans came after the Ethiopian revolution of 1974-75, when things took a serious turn there. These political upheavals did not drastically alter their economic situations for the worse; they came for political reasons not economic. So there is to my way of thinking very little empirical ground for talking about "economic migrants". The decisive reason behind the forced departure from their home country is inevitably a political event or development. Of course there is an economic element in most cases, but the point, which I find it important to make, is that there are extremely few cases where one could truly say that the cause of the flight was purely economic. The motives are intermingled, as they are in real life!

Unlike Africa and the other regions of the Third World the industrialized democracies have not reached any kind of consensus on how to define a *de facto* refugee. One of the reasons for this is the kind of discussion, which I have just dwelt on. Another is that the rich countries unlike the developing ones, had already some time ago enacted legislation in order to control immigration, which they have more or less adapted to deal with refugees. Every country, its legal establishment and the politicans conservatively tend to defend their own legislative and administrative traditions, so that even when amendments are enacted they are not done with the view of harmonizing their law and practice with those of other countries. Therefore there is in the rich countries no agreement on how to define or treat a *de facto* refugee, nor on which country should be responsable for refugee determination or for the protection and assistance of the refugee in those cases where an asylum-seeker has passed through several possible countries which might offer asylum. This has given rise to a new problem of so-called refugees in orbit. There are hundreds, some say thousands, of safety-seekers in Western Europe alone who over long periods are sent back and forth between countries, spending their time in prisons, interrogation rooms, and transit halls of airports. The latest cry is fear of all asylum-seekers arriving without any document. Harsh measures are being recommended, instead of, for example, reaching a European agreement, which could solve the problem without violating the rights of the asylum-seekers.

Within the Council of Europe there is a Committee *ad hoc* on Asylum and Refugees,(CAHAR) which holds regular meetings behind closed doors. Under prevailing conditions it is not surprising that this body has in secrecy arrived at a stand still. Other efforts under the auspices of the UNHCR have also produced little beyond paying lip service to the ideals.

The lack of joint Western European solutions does not mean that most of the countries have not found ways in their practice, and in some cases in their legislation, to give asylum to at least some categories of *de facto* refugees. But the difference from one country to another has created insecurity among the asylum-seekers and a lack of faith between the states concerned.

In the cold year of 1987

I have argued on these pages as I have on so many other occasions that refugees shall be recognized, protected and assisted and that realism as well as humanitarianism require that we apply the widened refugee definition as it was first developed in Africa. If that is done it will be easier to discern other categories of uprooted, displaced persons in like situations, so that they too can be in the position to plead to the World Conscience and be granted their full human rights, including the basic necessities and dignities of life.

I will conclude by taking a critical view on the political realities of today.

Foreign labour or, if we accept the expression, economic migration, is a very different thing from refugee movements. However urgent the conditions, it is the decisions of a free will that is found behind the departure from the home country of the migrant of the first kind, the foreign labourer. The refugee is forced to leave and in most cases lives thereafter with the hope of returning home one day when it is safe to do so. To what extent a country shall admit foreign labour and other forms of voluntary immigration is a matter to be decided exclusively by that country. The duty to receive refugees and to give them protection and fair treatment follows from international law, sometimes directly binding for the State in the legal sense, sometimes more in the moral or political sense.

Some say that we live in the era of the Bomb and the Migrant. I would say it is the era of the refugee as very few states today encourage anything but marginal immigration and then exclusively in the interest, as it is understood, of that State.

The overwhelming majority of the refugees originate in the Third World. The direct causes of their flight are conflicts kept alive mostly by super-power politics and by weapons forged and manufactured at bargain prices in the rich countries, who export death and destruction, and import the natural and partly processed products of the poor countries. At the same time they refuse to a great extent to receive the refugees who try to escape the suffering and the sorrow generated by super-power politics.

As I pointed out earlier an estimated 97 % or the majority of the refugees remain in the Third World countries. The rich countries in the West have started in the 1980s to defend themselves against immigration. It is not only Great Britain, who as John Galbraith pointed out, was once very busy defending its Empire and is now even more busy defending itself against that same Empire. All the rich countries of the West have embarked on something that I find best described as an arms race against humanitarianism. With a battery of measures they try to stop the safety-seekers and others moving between countries and even leaving their own. These measures include 1. Introducing visa and other permission-requirements from aliens before they are allowed to pass the border; 2. Pre-screening devices; 3. Secret and open diplomacy in countries of origin as well as countries of transit; 4. Harsh economic and other measures against airline-companies and other transporters if they carry passengers without the necessary visas and other documented permissions; 5. Introducing punishments and penalties for those who assist the asylum-seekers and others with or without payment; 6. Having government officials and other authorities distributing, with the assistance of uncritical mass-media misleading information. Expressions like "illegal migrants", "mass influx", "invasions of asylum-seekers", and "economic migrants" etc. are all designed to blow up and increase attitudes of xenophobia and racism; 7. The creation of forms for refugee-reception in centres and settlements and, through procedures including arrest and separation of families, which, whether governments admit it or not, will have the effect of deterring the refugee. The list can be prolonged, but these are probably the most important devices. The correctness of comparing these measures to an "arms race" becomes clear when one considers how this development forces one country after another to follow suit in this escalation of unilateral measures against refugees. As it is now one country cannot open its door even a fraction because it would then be alone in experiencing the entire pressure. Only in international co-operation and solidarity can we come back to a situation where it is possible to tear down these walls and decide again on quotas, assistance to refugees in their proper first countries of asylum and, above all, seek to put a stop to the violations of human rights, to warfare and to exploitation. The present situation is immoral. It is also dangerous because in the countries who practise these restrictions, it will in the long run lead to political conflicts and serious polarizations of the internal debate. It promotes military violence and police repression and it widens the gap of understanding and respect between the peoples of the Earth. It is very, very shortsighted.

The World needs change, new thinking and new people. Migration is change because it brings the new. What is good in the old will survive the change. What is bad I hope will not. In the meantime we must continue our work for Human Rights and respect for all beings.

Selected references

Collections of International Legal Instruments:

Collection of International Legal Instruments concerning Refugees, 2nd ed., UNHCR, Geneva 1979.

UN Resolutions and Decisions relating to the Office of the UNHCR, Doc. HCR/INF/48/ Rev. 3 with addenda.

G. Melander & P. Nobel, ed.: International Legal Instruments on Refugees in Africa / Instruments légaux internationaux sur les réfugiés en Afrique, bilingual ed., Scandinavian Institute of African Studies, Uppsala 1979.

Publications by UNHCR, Geneva:

Handbook on Procedures and Criteria for Determining Refugee Status under the 1951 Convention and the 1967 Protocol relating to the Status of Refugees, 1979

Declaration de Cartagena, trilingual ed. in Spanish, French and English, 1985.

The periodical *Refugees*.

Publications by the International Institute of Humanitarian Law, San Remo:

Report of the Working Group on Current Problems in the International Protection of Refugees and Displaced Persons in Asia, 1981.

G.J.L. Coles: Problems arising from Large Numbers of Asylum-Seekers: A Study of Protection Aspects, 1981.

Conclusions de Séminaire sur le droit d'asile et le droit de réfugiés dans le pays Arabes, 1984.

Other Books:

A. Grahl-Madsen: *Territorial Asylum*, Stockholm, New York 1980.

"Transnational Legal Problems of Refugees," *1982 Michigan Yearbook of International Legal Studies*, Clark Boardman Co., New York.

G. Goodwin-Gill: *The Refugee in International Law*, Oxford University Press 1983.

P. Sieghart: *The International Law of Human Rights*, Clarendon Press, Oxford 1983.

W. Shawcross: *The Quality of Mercy* André Deutsch, London 1984

Salman Rushdie.

Minority Literatures in a Multi-Cultural Society[*]

Salman Rushdie

I should admit that I have had some difficulty in deciding what an address like this should be about. Part of this difficulty simply has to do with the unease that is felt by a writer of fiction when he is asked to speak directly without any of the disguises that fiction permits. Another part of my unease derives from the fact that I have no theory. I have no large or systematic theory to offer to you, and I suspect that you might expect me to have one. What I have is merely a series of observations some of which are literary, some of which are personal, some of a more public nature, and I thought that I would simply offer you these and hope that some greater coherence might emerge. Certainly, I can't imagine myself as being in any way prescriptive about how a writer in a multi-cultural, not to say a multi-racial environment ought to respond to that environment. It seems to me that there are environments, and there are writers, and they will collide in different ways. My unease has to do with recent news events. It seems clear to me that in various parts of the British Isles, in Brixton and Tottenham for example, events have somewhat overtaken academic discussion, and if we are not to retreat into a kind of aestheticism, it will be necessary somehow to look into the light of those fires. That is to say that the question of living in a racially and culturally mixed society has to be considered as well as questions of a more literary nature.

I will take a deep breath and begin talking about James Joyce, and not only James Joyce, but *Finnegans Wake* . On the opening page of *Finnegans Wake* there is a word that is two lines of print long.(bababadalgharaghtakamminarronnkonn-nronntonnerronntuonnthunntrovarrhounawnskawntoohoohoordenenthurnuk!).
It is an onomatopaeic description of the fall of Finnegan, who is also the mythological giant, Finn MacCool, and in another sense Adam, so the fall is also the fall of man. My purpose in beginning with the sound of the human race's departure from Paradise is primarily to point out what the polyglots will already

have found out, that this apparently nonsensical sounding word is in fact composed of fragments of words from many different languages, words which mean things like "storm" "cloud" "thunder" "crash" and the like. My own French permits me to make out the word "tonnerre" lurking in there. My Hindi leads me to suspect the word "badal" in there, meaning cloud. Anyway, you will have to believe me, that this word is the most multi-cultural word in the whole of English literature, so let us consider it to be an open sesame or abracadabra, both of which, incidentally, are also words borrowed from other tongues to enrich this one. What I am trying to work my way round to saying is that in literature, cultural cross-fertilization is nothing very new. William Shakespeare, if I may now drag him in here, sets plays variously in Denmark, Verona, Venice, Troy, Rome, Alexandria, a mythical seacoast in Bohemia, and in the case of *Pericles* dispersedly in various countries, and in both theme and range of linguistic and cultural reference Shakespeare was the very opposite of the little Englander.

Indeed, from Shakespeare and onwards, when a work of literature has been "parochial," that is to say when it is judged to travel badly (I am thinking for example of the poetry of John Betjeman), to be of interest to nobody much outside the culture from which it springs, this is normally held to be a bad thing. It has been an important aspect of what it means to be a work of art that the work will cross frontiers. That is not to say that the work is specifically created for an international market; writers and artists are often, and possibly fortunately, unable to judge whether the work will find any audience at all beyond their close family members - let alone anywhere else. The intentions can be very confusing. I am reminded of an old Punch cartoon which depicts Leonardo da Vinci in his atelier surrounded by a group of rapt disciples, and what he is doing is holding the Mona Lisa by one corner of the canvas and hurling it across the room while he says: "Mark my words, one day men shall fly to Padua in such as these."

I am not talking so much about the writer's or the artist's intention, although such a writer as the American black writer Ralph Ellison explicitly stated his desire to connect what he loved in his own black experience with what he loved in the world beyond that experience. I am talking rather about the presence of something else, some quality in works of art that makes them of their essence multi-cultural in their potential or actual appeal. It is of course more or less impossible to say what this "whatness" is.

To return to Joyce, Stephen Dedalus says at one point that you can distinguish a horse from everything that is not horse, because a horse contains the quality of horseness. This is what makes all types of horse recognized as belonging to the same group. But what is horseness? Well, he is not defeated by this, "horseness," says Stephen "is the whatness of all horse." So artness is the whatness of all art, and I will say no more about it.

As an Indian by birth and upbringing I had access to a second literary tradition that was also culturally multiple. Ethnically, I belong to the group known as Kashmiri Muslims, not a very numerous group in India. But I am nevertheless pleased to think about such great non-Muslim Kashmiri works as for example the Nrityasahitya, in which in Sanskrit the principles of classical Indian dance were first laid down, or the wonderful animal fables of the Shantra Trantra, which also comes from Kashmir, or the extraordinary compendium of tales, which is longer than the Arabian Nights, called the "Ocean of the Streams of Stories." These are also part of my cultural heritage and a source of pleasure, in fact I found that my own instinct has led me more towards the kind of encyclopedia fictional quality of the "Ocean of the Streams of Stories" rather than to the delicacy of the Mogul or Muslim miniature. So perhaps I may say a bit more about these instincts, which have led me towards a more or less conscious strategy of eclecticism and mixtures. Talking for a moment about the classical sequence of Indian paintings known as the Hamzanama, that is to say ."the adventures of Hamza", a figure who may or may not be equatable with the historical character Hamza, who was the uncle of the Prophet Mohammed. They are remarkable pictures in many ways, not least for the way in which they destroy the myth that the Indian painting tradition is somehow transcendent and serene; they are extremely violent paintings, giants get speared in the brain, people get cut in half, frequently sections of limbs are removed and then laid out for inspection. So, if anybody holds the idea that India is somehow a mystical and peaceful culture, I strongly recommend that they look at these pictures. Even more extraordinary is the manner in which these great paintings were made. What happened was that the painters were assembled at the Mogul court from all over India, painters working in all the different styles of India, from the south to the north to the east to the west, and they were then required to collaborate on the canvasses, so perhaps one painter would do the figures, one would do the mosaic floor, a third would do the Chinese-looking sky with abstract calligraphic clouds which many of the paintings contain, and the result is this extraordinary group of paintings, in which the multiple nature of Indian culture, its plurality, its lack of homogeneity becomes the theme. They are paintings which give people who look at them what I call important kinds of permission, so that they say, "look, you can join this with this, and you would have thought it does not work, but in actual fact, it does. You can put this style against that one in the same painting, and it is ok." That is to say, there are no longer hard, dividing cultural lines; you no longer have to keep things apart from other things. If you can find a way to make anything go, then anything goes. In a way what the Hamzanama offers to Indian artists is a freedom which is not unlike the one which, according to the British playwright Howard Brenton, Shakespeare offers to British playwrights, that is to say, he showed them that plays do not have to be one thing. A comic scene could be followed by a tragic scene, and an intimate love story could be political. This cultural mixture, this cultural impurity, is certainly of great importance to me as a writer, but I repeat, this is nothing new, I am even coming to suspect that maybe this impurity is the norm in the history of cultures, and that notions of purity are the aberration - we know the little bit of trouble that was caused in Germany recently by such ideas. Actually, I have been beginning to suspect that there is no such thing as a homogeneous culture.

The urban Indian environment in which I grew up offered the most culturally mixed environment it is possible to imagine, and part of that mixture was, of course, Western, so that now when I get asked - as I do get asked - why I mingle eastern and western elements in my writing I find the answer perfectly obvious. In the first place both elements are mixed up inside me, because of where I have lived for a quarter of a century, and in the second place they were mixed up inside me in Bombay, long before I ever got to what we used to call "proper London."

The world of rural India is really no more homogeneous than the cities. Here too, old religions, Hindu and Islam, co-exist with new ones, intermediate technology and birth control. Pakistan, to which my family emigrated, is also a mess of cultures in conflict: immigrant bourgeoisie against the local bourgeoisie, North Indian culture versus the regional cultures, Urdu against the regional languages.

The homegrown cultures clash with each other too. Hindi against Punjabi, Punjabi against Maloach. It seems to me that I have been in minority groups all my life, a Muslim in India, immigrant in Pakistan and then in England. Now, of course, I find myself belonging to a seriously deprived culture whose entire way of life is threatened by the uncaring attitude of the majority, that is to say, writers. Sometimes I wonder what it must be like to be in the majority, for most people to look and think the same way as myself. On the whole I conclude it must be a terrible fate. I prefer the idea of being exceptional. But then perhaps we are all members of exception groups. If you look at any majority group it very quickly disintegrates into for example yoga fanatics, old people, dartplayers, Madonna fan clubs, football hooligans, advertising executives, corrupt policemen and gentlemen burglars, politicians, people who can do the Times' crosswords in under twenty minutes, gays, nude models, manufacturers of plastic bullets, librarians, and coal miners. So all societies are at least multi-sub-cultural, and most of us belong to more than one of this infinite variety of sub-cultures. Even the issue of migration is more complex than it seems. There is a sense in which all urban culture is migrant culture. Relatively few of the people who live in a major city were born there, and it may be that the journey from a remote Scottish village to London is in some way longer than a journey from another comparable metropolis, such as Bombay. It is true, however, that the cultural mix of the United Kingdom has been greatly enriched - though other people might use different verbs - in the last few decades by immigration from its former colonies. To the country's old and distinguished reputation as a place of refuge, which sheltered figures as disparate as Peter the Great and Karl Marx and which still permits for example erstwhile leaders of the Shah of Iran's torture-police to remain in the country, there has been added a new and ungenerous reputation of racial bigotry, a reputation, I would say, as well deserved as the other one. The effect on English literature - and on the arts of Britain generally - of these new voices promises to be profound. We must remember too that not all the immigrants come from ex-colonial backgrounds. Writers like Kazus Ishiguro or the Anglo-Chinese novelist Timothy Mo bring their own flavour into the literature of England. For some decades now the new literatures in the old empire have been offering up a body of work which England or even America would be hard put to equal: Patrick White, Christina Stead, Nadine Gordimer, André Brink, V.S. Naipaul, Derek Walcott, Amos Tutuola, Wole Soyinka, Chinua Achebe, R.K. Narayan, Anita Desai. It is quite a list. But in some of these countries, in particular those in which English is not the leading language, it seems to me that the flourishing of an English language writer is somehow a random event, that is to say, it does not come out of any great bubbling mass of writers. That seems to be the mark of the sub-structure, no constant pressure of work from which an occasional major figure emerges. In this respect the literature of black Britain may eventually come to be healthier than many of the new literatures outside Britain, for example India, because in Britain English is the prime language, the second and third generation born British kids more or less choose it as their medium of expression, and I think that there is now beginning to be the kind of swell of work from which artists of quality emerge.

I am trying now to move on to touch on some of the aspects of writing in a multi-racial society. It is clear from both the American and the British experience that being black in a predominantly white society has imposed upon many writers a kind of public responsibility, a kind of public project, which may be described as "giving voice." This has to do with speaking what is not spoken, with naming what is not named, with articulating a body of rejected knowledge; that is to say knowledge which is known to be true within the black world, but which is rejected by its white shadow. This "giving voice" can be subdivided into two further kinds of work, one of which you might say is anthemic, which is telling one's own people in songs or stories what they find pleasing or beautiful, what they know to be true. Here the work joins with the reader in the celebration of what the writer and the reader share. If outsiders wish to enter the world of the work, that is fine, but no particular concession has to be made to them. This is a kind of literature that bears witness, and if I may use an American example, the work of a writer such as Maya Angelou seems to fall into this category.

The other kind of "giving voice" is aimed more directly at the white community, and it becomes an exercise in shouting across what I have previously described as "a gulf in reality", the chasm which exists between white and black perceptions of the world, their mutual world. It seems to me that the project of "giving voice" necessitates a new language and a new kind of form. I don't believe that it is sufficient only to alter one's rhythms and accents, it seems to me that much more fundamental alterations need be made in the syntax and the content of the language if it is to be allowed to say new things. There are now projects which attempt to re-write history, to re-tell stories, which for too long have been in the hands of colonial powers. History has been described as an interview with winners. Part of the project of "giving voice" is to speak up for the great mass who never had the chance to sit down at a table, let alone to win, and this is clearly a literature of the highest importance and value. I do, however, have certain worries about the creation of a self-consciously black literature. That has to do for one thing with the assumed marginalization. I was once told by a British academic, who I suppose should be nameless, that it must be much easier for me to write as I do because I came from the periphery. The point about the periphery is that it implies a centre, and the idea of that centre still being in Hampstead was so bizarre that it was impossible to reply.

There will be, and I think there is an attempt by much of the established literary world to place this new writing in the margin of what they still believe to be the centre or the mainstream. I sometimes think that the invention of the term Commonwealth Literature is a part of this process of marginalization. The Commonwealth, or Commonwealth Literature, is a very strange beast, for example it contains South Africa and Pakistan who are not members of the real Commonwealth, but it excludes Britain which when last observed was a member, although an extremely badly behaved one. It can all too easily appear that the separation of this kind of literature from English literature is an attempt to preserve, to protect the study of writers less interesting than those on the periphery, less interesting writers but with far more academic work invested in them. What is particularly strange about Commonwealth Literature is that I have never yet encountered a writer who agreed that he or she was a member of this remarkable school. Is it not strange that a kind of writing should be taught in schools and colleges, when all its practitioners deny that they are in fact practising it. What can be created is a sense of marginalization, and often this will be well motivated, for example Commonwealth Literature students will explain that this writing would simply be squeezed out if it was grouped in with mainstream English literature, there simply would not be funds made available to study it, so it is off to the ghetto instead.

There is also, there seems to me, a danger of marginalization from within. In any group that sees itself - with good reason - as being on the defensive there is a risk that new orthodoxies will be erected. According to these new orthodoxies, for example, works which do not speak to us only, to the inside, become suspect; that is to say, parochialism instead of being considered a weakness becomes a virtue. Defensive walls which are erected around the culture can have the effect of crushing the literature inside it as well as keeping hostile forces out. This internal marginalization also seeks implicitly to control the writer's choice of subject matter. He must choose to write about the great public issues, that is to say there is pressure to write politically or he is not important, not, if I may use the term, pure. The use of ideas of homogeneity and purity by the majority white culture can easily create such mirror images in the beleaguered minority groups.

A third danger for the minority group writer, especially for the writer starting out on his career, is paranoia. I remember when I was twenty-one and beginning to write - I was in Pakistan then, having just left the university - I found it more or less impossible to write there because of the existence of total censorship. My problem with censorship was not so much ideological, although it was there too, it was more that I could never get a straight response to my work. I could never properly evaluate what I was doing. It is not unglamorous to have one of your first pieces of writing banned by the state, it makes you feel like a pretty wonderful writer. However, when people praise you you can't be sure which party line they are or are not toeing, and when they criticize you the same applies and so it becomes impossible to learn. I came back to England to try to overcome this problem, and although I would agree that England is by no means Paradise, the situation there did not seem to me to be comparable to the one I had left. For some people, however, the British response to their work does feel as suspect as I found the Pakistani one. The problem of paranoia is of course most acute when people are actually persecuting you, and in the context of a racist society it is very seductive to lean on one's otherness and sometimes to use it as an excuse. Good writers do not, obviously, do this, but others do. I would like to stress that I am not really speaking against the need for black voices to find their own language, their own style or their own methods. What I am doing is stating my own shifting solutions to these issues, rehearsing the struggle that takes place more or less constantly inside myself, so my own solutions probably make sense to nobody but myself, but they are at the moment these: I do not believe that I write for an audience, which is not to say that I am unaware of the existence of one, but rather that I really don't know how to write to please an audience. I know that as a reader myself I resent the feeling in a book that the writer is somehow playing to the audience, or playing to the gallery, that is to say, me. I do not wish to be played to, pandered to in that way as a reader, and therefore as a writer I try not to do it. I write, I suppose, for the idea, to bring it out of nothing, to shape it, to make it work, to make it do as much work as possible, and God knows that is hard enough. And because we are talking about fiction, after all, it appears to my mind that the business of making a novel is the business of making a world, and I believe that if the world is properly made then it feels true to any reader who picks it up. The reader can enter the world and feel happy with it whether or not he knows much about the real world on which the book is based. I have never been to Africa or South America, but it does not prevent me from reading their books. I can go there through the literature and feel with no personal evidence that what I am reading is in some imaginative sense the truth, but this obviously does not mean that I see what an African or a South American reader would see, but it seems to me that I do see a lot.

I also insist on my right to choose my subjects anywhere, in any material, or rather, because that seems to be how it works, to be chosen by them. The idea of authenticity which I discussed has always, at least when it applies to non-white writers, carried with it a number of restrictions. An American writer is allowed to write about anywhere. If John Updike for example chooses to write a novel about Africa, that is accepted, it is not considered unauthentic. However, it is often thought to be unauthentically Indian if for example R.K. Narayan was to set a novel in America. So the idea of authenticity creates restrictions, the Indian writer must write about India, and I suppose a black British writer must write about the black British experience.

I recall years ago seeing an interview with James Berry in which he said that one of the most dangerous side-effects of racism is that black writers spend all their time thinking that they should write about the white man, when they might merely wish to write about everything writers want to write about: love, death, money, the whole business of being human. I hold, I suppose, a similar view. That is to say, my writing has always arisen fairly directly out of the circumstances of my life. In the book I am now writing, the theme of migration is an essential one. I am not seeking to make an attempted withdrawal from my race or from my position in history, but I do want to reach, like Ralph Ellison did, beyond that to all the things I worry about, like hatred and love, which have nothing to do with my ethnicity.

If I may return for a moment to Tottenham. I have been going to Tottenham for many years to follow the local football club, and it seems to me that I would like to be free to write about this extraordinary and wonderful football club as well as - or even instead of - the Tottenham of the riots. This is not necessarily a matter of right or wrong, it is more a matter of temperament; many fine writers may feel that their writing is done on behalf of an audience, on behalf of their people. I simply resist the idea of being representative. I think one of the difficulties of writers in our position that we may wish to discuss is this: if you know a community by virtue of being a member of it then you know it, warts and all. If you seek honestly to portray it that is how the portrait will come out. This at once lays you open to the serious charge of lending ammunition to your enemies, of offering up negative images of your own people within the context of a prejudiced society. It should be noticed that this charge can be levelled at writers, even the community they belong to cannot really be said to be under threat. Much of New York's Jewish establishment attacked Philip Roth for having written an anti-semitic novel called *Portnoy's Complaint* . Is it right that a writer should be asked to provide his community with role models, culture heroes, shining images and avoid all mention of warts. Many would say that in certain historical situations it is. I disagree. There is a new film, written by the British/Asian writer Hanif Kureishi, that raises some of these issues, so I thought I might discuss it briefly. This film is called *My Beautiful Laundrette* . It tells the story of an Asian school leaver, Omar, known to his mates as Omo after a brand of washing powder that claims to wash clothes whiter. Omar's father, who is an alchoholic, asks his successful businessman brother to give Omar some sort of a job. Omar starts washing cars in his uncle's garage, but soon becomes manager of a decrepit laundrette, which he jazzes up and turns into a great success. He renames it "Powders" and plays canned music etc. It could be an everyday story about life in Thatcherite Britain except that the Thatcherites are Asian. Omar's uncle is a slum landlord, and when one of his black tenants complains about being evicted, yelling that Asians should not treat blacks in this way, the uncle replies: "I am not a professional Asian, I am a professional businessman." Much of the film offers an extremely sharp and well-written satire of the life style of London's Asian fat cats, and already before the film's commercial release there had been protests about its unfairness to the Asian community. The point is that the satire rings true, but in spite of this there is a point of view which says that it should simply not be undertaken. These things should not be discussed, just as for example the treatment of Asian women by Asian men should not be discussed, or the divisions within the Asian community or the black community should not be discussed, or the recent unease felt about the bitterness between the black and Asian communities. I should say about this last subject that it seems to me recently to have been headlines in the British press in the most suspect way, which does indeed give rise to feelings that a kind of divide-and-rule approach is in the air.

My Beautiful Laundrette is very far from being some kind of nihilistic sneer, it is funny, touching, passionate, to my mind one of the finest works of art to emerge from the new generation of black British writers, and I think that a substantial part of its quality has to do with the writer's courage, his decision simply to say what he sees and stand by it. The film's central relationship is between Omar and a white ex-school friend, called Johnny, who has flirted with fascism, but who actually loves Omar. The love of these two is presented very explicitly and is both extremely sensual and very moving. It is not often that a film love affair looks like an adult relationship, but this one manages to do just that, and it is also of course a metaphor of hope. The relationship is subject to colossal stresses, both from the Asian and the white side. Johnny's former fascist friends smash up the laundrette and beat him up, but the film ends with the love surviving, literally bloodied, but surviving. There is a kind of heroism, but it is not the kind of heroism which will satisfy people who want positive images of blacks. I doubt that a community as sexually silent and conservative as the Asians would take kindly to a gay hero who makes love to a former National Front member. I would defend *My Beautiful Laundrette* against all colours, even though it will upset some Asians. In fact there are some fat cat Asian businessmen that I would not mind upsetting. Even though, more seriously, some white viewers will find in it material which will satisfy their wish to dislike Asians - in the film for example all the Englishmen are poor and all the Asians are rich and this creates resentment, I suppose. The reason for my defence is that there is nothing in it that is imaginatively false, and because it seems to me that the real gift which we can offer our communities is not the creation of a set of stereotyped positive images to counteract the stereotyped negative ones, but simply the gift of treating black and Asian characters in a way that white writers seem very rarely able to do, that is to say as fully realized human beings, as complex creatures, good, bad, bad, good. To do anything less is to be kept captive by the racist prejudices of the majority, and that complexity is what Kureishi's script strives for.

It would, however, be like hiding your head in the sand if one only considered literature at this point in history when social riots are raging through the inner cities of Britain. The British Government sees the riots as a law and order issue. After all, the Conservative Party's new deputy chairman, the distinguished novelist Geoffrey Archer, has recently vouchsafed that unemployment is the fault of the unemployed. If this is so it cannot be used to explain why they riot. People who do not work because they do not wish to work cannot, obviously, simultaneously point to the unemployment as a source of discontent. They should be happy. If they are not, it is because they are criminal. It is because they are in the grip of drug barons, it is because they are stirred up by outside agitators, it is because liberal and permissive types have created the climate in which the rioters think that it is OK to riot. It is because blacks are excitable and emotional and therefor more prone to rioting than phlegmatic cold-country whites. All the above sentiments have been uttered by several persons, and in places as august as the columns of *The Times* in the last few weeks. I am reminded of the end of the film *Casablanca* where a cynical police chief, trying to cover up the facts, tells his men to round up the usual suspects. Meanwhile, firebomb attacks on black and Asian families have become almost daily events. Racial harassment in general is very sharply on the increase. The behaviour of the police towards the ethnic minorities, far from being condemned, is praised by the government and they are promised plastic bullets, indeed any equipment they might feel they need. I am the most timid of men, I can't imagine myself picking up, much less throwing a petrol bomb, but I suspect many of the people who rioted would have described themselves in just such terms. Strange things happen at the breaking point. Even steel bars snap, and I think that in Britain's inner cities it is self-evident that that breaking point was reached. Now you have black communities all over the country who are not just angry, but afraid. A black youth in Tottenham asked his TV interviewer: "Would you even be talking to me if it wasn't for the riots?" But in contemporary Britain, in its conservative press, which is another term for the national press, the views of the ethnic minorities still get heard with some difficulties. Occasionally they are heard, but the volume of what is said from the other side deafens, I suspect, almost everybody except the already converted. A country that refuses to listen to its most threatened, most disadvantaged, and most frightened citizens until they start running through the streets burning things, is a culture which creates the crisis which it then seems to deplore. I said at the beginning that I was not going to prescribe responses to history, and I don't intend to do so now. Some of us will wish in a situation such as this to leap in and join the fight, some of us may wish to wait cautiously for the fires to die down and then in the calm of the aftermath to try and say what they had meant to say or simply to weave them into our stories, and I don't think that these are mutually exclusive responses. However, the inescapable truth is that whatever our choices as writers, our texts are going to have to reckon with the disturbing context in which they must at the moment be made.

* This is an edited version of the opening speech given by Salman Rushdie at a conference held at Kungliga Svenska Vitterhedsakademien in Stockholm in October 1986.

The Products of Wealth

Peter Lyssiotis

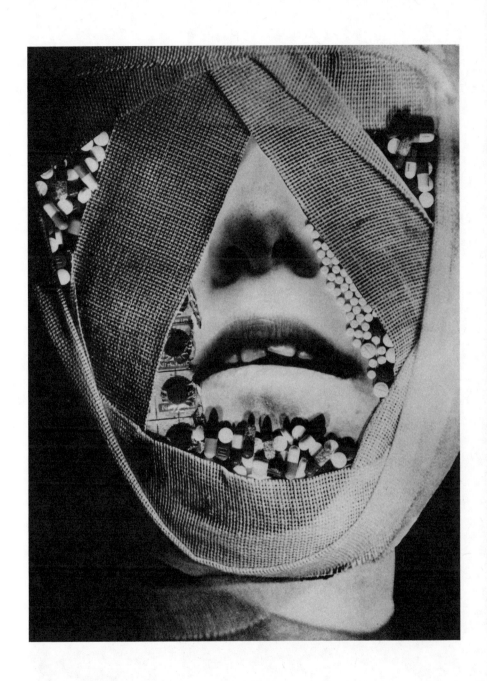

Migrants in the Sky

Philip Salom

At times, by endless concentration (you feel mad
and look it) it is possible to see their dreams.
It strikes by accident, a sudden jolt.
Or you go like a thief into the darkened house
but cannot lift a single object.
Perhaps you know them, and condescend, being
intellectual, being a sociologist, being well informed...
but they *are* the raw material.

                                             The century
falls apart and becomes, absurdly, this locus:
continental drift in the fractions
dreamt by these survivors, in detail down
to individual streets, the intensely-known rooms in houses.
Each dreamer wears a world
like a knock-down film set. Only they will survive it.

Some still wear the World War. Or a third world,
flame-filled. Red with sirens ... Some
climbed over the gunwhales off Vietnam.
Worlds whose power they can't escape,
an occult circle they cannot step from,
and inside a maniac whose embrace drains them.
Buildings crash down, their joints completely gone.
The old city, architecture, laboured stone:
a densely shattered music - what is culture but chords
compressed there by the thousand? Let go now,
gone into space. Their universe gapes, and will not
be filled by concrete.
Many came from peace, unstated
conflicts pushed them. Some simply came.

Intensities gather on them like on Gods.
They reassemble, and shift into the sky.
They won't know their adopted cities, for all the years
they live in them. There are always these impossible
cities of the past. Steel and glass, the long
undifferentiated face of clamour..? No. They will not.

You look and turn away. You put the parts
together, make an intellectual structure of it,
one for each of them if you're generous;
one for all of them, more usually. Really, it's for you.
You may feel their second pulse, the heart-felt
intuition of the listener. Your face curls into emotion.

So to live in a young country without being brash.
You've never been on the outer. This dissolution
of the ego shouldn't make you feel any better.

Beyond the echo:
migrant writing and Australian literature

Sneja Gunew

> To find our measure, exactly,
> not the echo of other voices.
> (Antigone Kefala)[1]

What are some of the implications if one includes migrant writing in any consideration of Australian literature?

The recently published *Oxford Companion to Australian Literature* [2] includes an entry on feminism and one on Aboriginal writing but nothing under "migrant", "ethnic", or multicultural writing, though it does have entries for some individual writers who are often conjured up under those terms. Leonie Kramer's massive two-volume anthology *My Country* [3] includes a tiny handful of non Anglo-Celtic writers as part of that general chorus affirming "literary excellence" who have been selected by an absolute and mysterious process.

What might migrant writing offer that is not already covered by the traditional canon? How does one interrogate those unacknowledged forces which consign some (even after several generations) to the margins of a culture? And what does it mean, conversely, to claim to speak or write from a position "outside" Australian culture? Claiming legitimation or authority on the basis of geographical and historical accidents remains unconvincing and is akin to the trap of biological determinism which argues that women write differently because they are born women. As Simone de Beauvoir argued many decades ago, it is always a case of having to *learn* how to be a woman. Similarly it could be argued that one learns to be a migrant in the sense that after the initial sheer struggle to survive one must reconstruct and analyse the experience of migration. Central to this selfconscious recognition of one's otherness is the issues of language: how one learns to describe oneself as a human being in both the outer public and the inner private world.

Generally speaking, in the matter of writing, we can take up a range of positions (often contradictory ones) within these various public and private texts. Questions of who writes and for whom are traversed by the historical specificities of gender, class, culture and all of these are fluid concepts. In a recent interview David Malouf states that we all inhabit many cultures and I would add that these vary in their implications from one moment to another for every person.[4] For example, as a member of an Australian academic culture what I write and how I am read changes considerably according to whether I live out this label within the familiar regional sub-group of being part of Victoria's youngest university or whether I am at an overseas conference representing "Australia". Language functions as a way of reflecting back a coherent and socially viable self and too bad about the untidy or excessive bits (including the selves projected by another language) which get left out of the mirror. To be human, according to classic psychoanalysis, means that we invariably experience those suppressions but in the socio-political arena the nature and degree of these suppressions is a differently contested area.

Here I return to that question of degrees of foreignness (when do I start/stop being a migrant?) and authenticity. Although we may not all be born women or migrants and theoretically anyone can take up these positions, nonetheless the subtle complexities of living as a woman, as a migrant, in a particular place and period have an involved material reality. How one lives in the world as woman, as a migrant, and how one is reflected back by the language of others and one's own, necessarily informs those positions. Theories which aim to change those positions beyond the oppressions of cultural stereotypes need to come (at least in part) from those who live out these positions. However well-meaning individuals who are the arbiters of cultural values may be, they need finally to share their power. They must allow the marginal to speak on their *own* behalf. Today, due in large part to the black movement as much as to feminism, we have become more alert to the dangers of psychic as well as physical colonization. Therefore it is crucial to give a space (Lebensraum/Sprechensraum/Schreibensraum) to those whose experiences emanate from marginalised groups. A woman, a migrant, a black, do not necessarily and automatically interrogate received opinion but it is only from them ultimately that new autorities of experience, beyond the stereotypes, will emerge.

The first wave of migrant writing offered perspectives on mainstream Australian culture which were either nervously approving (the overwhelming desire to be accepted) or often as clumsily disapproving (Australia as a cultural desert). At the same time these texts appealed to a community of readers from similarly alternative cultural systems (an impossible mesh of class, gender, religion, food, music, etc.) who were invited to reminisce about the old world and the old ways. Such appeals, when lived out in the social realm, often became oppressive to the next generation and were often in direct contradiction to values encountered here, for example, rules governing marriage and acceptable behaviour for women. But these writings also formed the base for questioning what was considered "natural" behaviour in this culture. What had been accepted as cultural orthodoxies became teased out into historically specific constructs. Why certain meanings became enshrined was revealed as a combination of both unconscious and manipulative, vested interests. This recognition makes change possible. The questioning contained in migrant writing ranges from content (catalogues of experience of prejudice and racism) to structure: *ways* of writing are opened up to other possibilities from other cultures.

Being open to these writings from outside the literary canon doesn't mean just adding another true-life story from the culturally disadvantaged. What it does mean is that we pay attention to the way a familiar language can behave in unfamiliar and innovative ways and do not dismiss it for doing so. The reflected selves, including familiar Australian selves, will be quite different if one doesn't simply discuss such texts as belonging to oral history or sociology: the unsophisticated voices of those struggling to learn "proper" English. Migrant writing from those whose culture and language is not primarily Anglo-Celtic is part of the "measure" of being Australian.

Multiculturalism redefined: Reading some migrant women writers in Australia

The term "migrant writers" has general currency in Australia alongside synonymous phrases such as "ethnic" or "multicultural" writers. In practice it marks a distinction between Australian writers who are Anglo-Celtic in their cultural affiliations and Australian writers who come from non-Anglo-Celtic backgrounds.[5] The latter, the non-Anglo-Celts are dubbed "migrant", "ethnic" or "multicultural". Most have a language other than English, some choose to write in it but what circulates generally as "migrant writing" in Australia is either written in English or has been translated into English. So migrant women writers here means women writing from non-Anglo-Celtic backgrounds, usually in English. Now what about the term "multiculturalism"?[6]

Before launching into this I should perhaps note that those who still see themselves as following the New Critical concept of the "verbal icon" might object here to the intrusion of what they might dub "extra-literary" concerns, that is, might object to bringing politics into literature. But, as Terry Eagleton has put it, "there is no way of settling the question of which politics is preferable in literary critical terms. You simply have to argue about politics."[7]

The birth of multiculturalism as a term marked a transition in Australian immigration policy from so-called assimilation (based on an assumption that Australia was a unified or monocultural society) to the acknowledgement that Australia was in fact a culturally diversified nation. In theory Australia was comprised of a whole range of diverse cultures which all had equal access to the way "culture" was constructed in the public sphere and to cultural funding as disseminated through the federal Australian Council and comparable state bodies. In theory! What is certainly clear at present, though one hopes that it will change in the future, is that multiculturalism in practice means something quite other than egalitarian cultural diversity. In practice the old hierarchies and values are still operating. For example, in the funding bodies I have mentioned there are very few people who come from non Anglo-Celtic backgrounds.[8] If one turns to other institutional infrastructures and looks at the way Australian literature and culture are defined in the public mode, for example, in the reviewing pages of daily newspapers or in journals, or, at such incarnations of "high culture" as *The Oxford History of Australian Literature*, then one discovers that "assimilation" is still the order of the day. In other words, few non-Anglo-Celtic writers are mentioned in *The Oxford History* and those who do appear are not differentiated in any way from the Anglo-Celts.[9] Assimilation signifies "the same" and this is precisely what happens: the non-Anglo-Celts are rendered the same as the Anglo-Celts. It reminds one a bit of the way women are turned into honorary men when they become successful because men are the norm, the positively marked term in such dichotomies.

Anglo-Celtic writing, in turn, is seen as deriving from the English tradition - an off-shoot of *British* Literature (it is only ever called *English* Literature of course) - which is part of the whole Anglicizing process that took place during the constitution and operation of the British Empire.[10] Cultural imperialism evidently outlasts political imperialism. This derivative nature of Australian Literature is camouflaged in two ways: either by invoking universal standards of excellence (never defined but all the more potent because of this. We are after all speaking of theology here rather than logic), or, secondly, it is camouflaged by invoking the dissident tradition within English Literature, that is provided by Irish Literature, which is constructed as radical, democratically-based, anti-authoritarian. Neither of these manoeuvres allows visibility to non-Anglo-Celts, though I must add here that the notion that there is only "good" and "bad" literature has certainly been internalised by a number of non-Anglo-Celtic writers who would like to believe in literature (or culture) as a pure realm of aesthetics which transcends politics. Quoting Terry Eagleton again:

> The task of the moral technology of Literature is to produce an historically peculiar form of human subject who is sensitive, receptive, imaginative and so on... *about nothing in particular.* [11]

Thus, of course, we have a subject who is a-political, or, as Eagleton goes on to say, "drastically depoliticised, and hence in thrall to the dominant social order".

Within the parameters which I have been sketching, multiculturalism has become an alibi of liberal humanism, in other words, a case of *plus ça change . ...* Those who control the public sphere[12] are *seen to be doing* the right thing. After all, officially, one third (or sometimes one half, it all depends which criteria you use) of the Australian population now have various kinds of affiliation with cultures other than the Anglo-Celtic ones. Under that schema, official multiculturalism is often reduced to nostalgia and folklore. In other words, it becomes a case of preserving languages and colourful customs (predominantly peasant customs, costumes, and cooking) while the first generation of immigrants are still alive. Eventually it will all die out because the kids aren't interested Anything which might *retain* the interests of the children, such as teaching them their own language or teaching them the literary tradition of their non-English countries, is very badly funded. Community languages are kept alive largely in weekend schools which are funded by the community itself rather than by the government.

That all writing should be studied in terms of the cultural backgrounds of both writers and readers in order to make manifest the processes whereby meanings are constructed is not yet a dominant or accepted critical method. Neither culture nor gender nor class nor race are yet seen as being generally relevant to the study of literary or any other cultural productions.

Insofar as migrant writing, or non-Anglo-Celtic writing, circulates at all in Australia it is within the areas of sociology and history. Both rely on first-person accounts because authentic actors or witnesses are required here. In sociology it is a matter of studying migrant problems and here the migrant is invariably constructed as an unskilled worker, or working class and disadvantaged. It's not that I'm saying that migrants don't have problems but rather that I'm resisting the sociological construction that migrants are seen as the problem, that they *embody* problems in this discursive formation. In history, the migrants are part of the impulse to incorporate oral history in order to democratise the history machine - they are targeted as another silenced and oppressed group, together with women, the working-class, the Aborigines. Again the authentic first-person account is the raw material, speech rather than writing and if writing, then in the sense of recorded speech.[13]

So to argue for *writing* from non-Anglo-Celts in terms of literature, or textuality, self-consciously crafted writing, is very difficult. And this is where multiculturalism needs to be redefined. If it is wielded as a way of breaking down hegemonies, the public sphere, monoculturalism, then it does have its uses and its theory of cultural equality, can be its practice. In this version the Anglo-Celts too would be seen as part of multiculturalism and there would no longer be the division between "ethnics" and Australians. It would simply be a case of *all* Australians being *hyphenated* Australians: Irish-Australian or Greek-Australian etc.

Now, to the question of migrant women's writing. Considering migrant women's writing in Australia means adding the complications of culture to those of class and gender. And it's not as though migrants or migrant women are totally absent from Australian writing as it is currently institutionalised. Migrants in general, and migrant women in particular, function as metaphors for the foreign, the alien, the other, in Australian writing. Very specifically they signify excessive sexuality; food, factory fodder, silence, and specifically the silence of the ghetto. In the face of these representations of migrant women which have been constructed by, in the main, Anglo-Celtic men, it is not surprising that migrant women writers often explicitly parody such stereotypes.[14]

One such parody of the so-called lucky country is provided by the work of Rosa Cappiello. There are no stiff upper lips in Rosa Capiello's *Oh Lucky Country*,[15] no Anglo-ethnic understatements. In fact, there are no stiff or solid boundaries anywhere in this novel which inflates migrant oppression to such absurdist proportions that in its very excessiveness it becomes a force for renewal and imaginative energy. Capiello, a former immigrant from Naples initially wrote the book in Italian. Unfortunately, as the introduction by the translator Gaetano Rando informs us, readers of the English version miss out on the word play and allusions which draw upon the Neapolitan dialect as well as on Italo-Australian.

What readers of the English do get, however, is a new voice within Australian writing.

Insofar as we hear migrant voices at all in Australian writing, we are accustomed to hearing them as victims, mostly silent and invisible, particularly in those first-person accounts which usually fall into the category labelled oral history. These accounts, duly reworked into the muted understatements acceptable to Anglo-Celtic ears evoke pity but a pity tinged with complacency. We mainstream readers are not prepared for this kind of extravaganza.

This outcast voice from the bottom, from the gutter, sets up a fermentation which boils over into a flood, an inundation which sweeps over all the clichés about being migrant. It does not spring from a vacuum but emerges from a tradition not often heard in Australian writing. One thinks of other celebrants of the outcast like Genét, Céline, Pasolini, and perhaps most centrally the grand-daddy of them all - Rabelais. In his seminal study of Rabelais, the Russian critic Mikhail Bakhtin describes this kind of writing, devoted to carnival and the grotesque, as being fundamentally subversive to accepted norms of the literary and the social. In carnival the world is turned upside down so, where better to locate it than in the antipodes. It also signals the reign of the body instead of the spirit. What better way to give philosophical respectability to Australia's much vaunted devotion to hedonism. Monstrous excess rules; the last shall be first, including women and migrants. As Bakhtin says:

> The grotesque body...is a body in the act of becoming. It is never finished, never completed.... Moreover, the body swallows the world and is itself swallowed by the world...[16]

Uyen Loewald's story "Silver Jubilee"[17] is one of the first examples of someone writing from a Vietnamese background. The story can be read as an allegory for the migrant condition: those who are handicapped, deprived of enabling speech, denied the social formation of subject identities, constructed by others and effaced by those constructions. As well it reveals strategies for resistance, covert resistances (not on a grand scale) for those who inhabit the minority and exist on sufferance.

Nonetheless, such strategies are uncomfortable for others (Kew dresses in rags, thus denigrating her family's public reputation and she refuses the wifely role of cook). The story can also be read in the current sense of post-modernist "narrative allegory" which Geoffrey Ulmer describes as favouring "the material of the signifiers over the meanings of the signifieds."[18] He relates this to techniques of montage and collage, processes of interruption and re-ordering, which draw attention to the *materiality* of representation; in this case language and within it the *code* of gender, culture etc. In a recent seminar in Melbourne the film critic Laura Mulvey argued that those who have been denied an expression of personal memory, or denied participation in the formulation of the public languages of history, culture etc., construct a new political rhetoric that is often dependent on gesture, metaphor and allegory. Thus when Kew pulls down the tablecloth and its feast she is demolishing the foundations of the family which traps her in its construction of her as a redundant, superfluous, silent old woman.

Ania Walwicz and Antigone Kefala: Varieties of migrant dreaming.

Literature remains the currency in use in a society apprised, by the very form of words, of the meaning of what it consumes.
(Barthes, *Writing degree Zero*)[19]

How easy is it, even now, to attach notions of the literary to migrant writing? If not, then what are the implications if migrants wish to participate in selecting the words which, according to Barthes, consolidate social meaning? What kind of signification is migrant writing permitted within Australia?

As we have noted, we often deal under this rubric not with writing produced by migrants so much as writing by others on behalf of migrants. In any case, such writing is not usually received as literature which, for the moment, we will describe as a textuality which is visibly more worked over than other forms of writing and whose implicit opposite is the apparent "disorder" of speech.[20] If we accept the suggestion that migrant writing signifies only within the formations of sociology and history then, paradoxically, its value lies here with speech rather than writing. In other words, the migrant's speech (rather than writing) is solicited and the more disordered it is the more authentic it supposedly sounds. In those terms migrant writing is valued precisely insofar as it is inscribed with the marks of linguistic naivety and (even) incompetence: broken language being symptomatic of subjects not yet assimilated (rendered the same) or 'naturalized'.

In the face of the little writing which does get limited exposure (autobiographical or autobiographically based) any obvious signs of language being crafted are nonetheless read as relatively unmediated confessions. Complexities, if acknowledged, are those provided by life, the complicated history of the migrant subject, rather than any consciously wrought textuality. Therefore, to consider migrant poetry is, under those circumstances, perverse. Poetry, the least transparently functional manifestation of linguistic self-consciousness, will be read with difficulty for sociological or historial content. In Barthes' terms, classical poetry is "a speech which is made more socially acceptable by virtue of the very conspicuousness of its conventions."[21] To write poetry means that one is staking a claim to the literary and hence to public cultural participation. On what grounds can this be legitimated, more particularly when the language used is patently either not English, or, if English, then filtered through a previous and other language? Those "conspicuous conventions", alluded to by Barthes, are not simply acquired when setting foot on this continent, nor are they part of the naturalization certificate. Rather, they belong to that chimeric cultural superstructure which floats above the home territory signifying a mystery only gradually comprehended after many rites of passage. Poetry? From migrants? Classic realist narratives perhaps, and reluctantly, but not poetry. Nevertheless, we are faced here with the poetry of Ania Walwicz and Antigone Kefala.

To some extent, as I have argued elsewhere,[22] the experience of migration, particularly when it involves negotiating another language, changes the conditions which make signification possible. In some ways, and speaking largely metaphorically, it may be seen as analogues to re-entering the symbolic,[23] or, in classic Freudian terms, with changing the secondary, censoring processes of the preconscious.[24] In either model we are dealing with a foundation process in the construction of human subjectivity, with the conditions under which subjects both participate in and are produced by signification. Entering language means becoming a social being rescued from the incoherence and anarchy of drives ("the mental representative of a somatic impulse"[25]) but at the cost, inevitably, of certain repressions, including degrees of alienation from the drives.[26]

In no sense does this linguistic and psycho-analytic model support the concept of a unified or sovereign subject who is the origin of meaning. More appropriately one thinks of subject positions: a series of statements (distinguishing between a speaking subject and spoken subject[27]) appealing in various ways to a community of addressees or readers. These interactions are complicated amongst other things by history, by gender, by culture.[28]

In the last few decades there have been considerable efforts to mark the discursive formation of Australian literature, in gendered and cultural terms, as predominantly Anglo-Celtic and male. As a reaction to this we have those people who consider the implications of Aboriginal writing (oral, colonised[29]) and women's writing (throwing new light, for example, on foundation myths of mateship and the bush[30]). What further complications result when one inserts migrant women poets? At the very simplest level this means that any language cannot be considered transparent or referential in the fullest sense, that is, offering direct access to the phenomenal or physical world. Those who are able to think from the beginning in more than one language find it impossible to consider language as a 'natural' and unproblematic expression of experience. Neither does this hold true for those who have experience of more than one culture (and we are probably dealing with a question of degree here) for here too it is difficult to accept culture as 'natural'.[31] Furthermore, neither migrants nor women should be lumped together into non-specific homogeneity.[32] Insofar as gender and writing will be considered in this paper, I do not believe that the possession of a womb is automatically and mystically figured or inscribed in textualities. Not being, but living as a woman, historically and materially, necessarily informs one's writing. The contradictions expressed here are more precisely formulated by Juliet Mitchell:

> Literary forms arise as one of the ways in which changing subjects create themselves as subjects within a new social context. The novel is the prime example of the way women start to create themselves as social subjects under bourgeois capitalism - create themselves as a category: women...I believe that it has to be the discourse of the hysteric. The woman novelist must be an hysteric. Hysteria is the woman's simultaneous acceptance and refusal of the organisation of sexuality under patriarchal capitalism. It is simultaneously what a woman can do both to be feminine and to refuse feminity, within patriarchal discourse. And I think that is exactly what the novel is; I do not believe there is such a thing as female writing, a "woman's voice". There is the hysteric's voice which is *the woman's masculine language* (one has to speak "masculinely" in a phallocentric world) talking about feminine experience.[33]

So to Walwicz and Kefala. Broadly speaking, the subject positions constructed in Walwicz's prose poems reproduce or re-enact the linguistic and social contradictions which construct migrant subjects. Her approach to language is to replicate its semi- or unconscious shaping powers. Thus the incantatory and repetitious style of her texts. Kefala's poetry, on the other hand, invites rational analysis of the contradictory nature of migrant positions. While Walwicz' work covers over the gap between "I" and "you" and encourages the reader's identification with the narrator, Kefala's narrator remains separate and appeals both to a community of readers with shared cultural dislocations as well as extending an invitation to Anglo-Celtic readers to understand these predicaments. Walwicz is confrontational; Kefala consensual.[34]

Ania Walwicz arrived here from Poland when she was 13. Her poetry is characterized by simple language and hypnotic repetition designed to be most effective as performance poetry.[35] The prevailing associative logic is familiar to us from dreams, or, at least, from the tradition of surrealist writing. Displacement and condensation are the governing devices: similar words and contiguous words structure the poems.[36]

A cluster of poems deal with the first contacts with the new culture and offer variations on the trope of parent-child reversals. The parents grow increasingly smaller under the pressures of alien social processes and rely on their children to negotiate the social apparatus. The children, in time, disappear under this burden.

We were so big there and could do everything. When you have lots you know it. Lucky and lucky and money. My father was the tallest man in the world. Here we were nothing. There vet in the district and respect. The head of the returned soldiers and medals. Here washed floors in the serum laboratory. Shrinking man. I grow smaller every day. The world gets too big for me. We were too small for this big country. We were so little. We were nothing. We were none and naught and no money. We were no speak. There we were big and big time. Here we were so little. Hardly any. We grew tiny. Scared lost not knowing how to speak. At the mercy of other people to put us up. We didn't amount to much. There I was good at school. Here they put me in a grade lower. We grew smaller in height. We were reduced. We had a smaller areas. Before we had a house. And here we had only one room to be in. I had big ideas before and here I didn't know how to say what I wanted to be. Was no one and nothing at all. I didn't belong anywhere. I was hardly here. Waiting for people to pick me up after school. And I forgot my address and wouldn't know what to say to anybody. And if they didn't pick me up I'd stand there all night and wouldn't know what to do at all. I was so small. The shower was too big for me. When you have plenty you can be kind. Father goes away. Mother goes away. They had room to move. Now we didn't have any. We were put in a box. We are so poor and all together. I used to think how nice that could be. But it wasn't nice. And we were at one another. We turned on one another. And quarrelled. And I ran away. And he ran away. And I didn't go to school one day. And we went to the golf links. And sat on a bench and escaped. And I got cold and stayed in bed. And I was unhappy. And we were lost. And he could not do his job. And had to pass exams. And we didn't have any money. And the landlord came. Two little girls hid under the bed. He saw through the window and felt sorry. I had to be old early and ashamed of what happened. We are going to travel he said. Your name will be Anne. Your name will be Mary. I was hoping they'd catch us near the border. But they didn't. And we travelled in the white snow that was nowhere. And in the blue ocean that was nowhere. To get to a place where we were less and had less and were less and less and grew smaller every day.[37]

The poem begins by invoking the childhood fantasy that parents particularly fathers, are all-powerful and confer these privileges, by extension, to the whole family ("we were so big there and could do everything"). In the oneiric logic of condensation, the shrinking father shrinks the child narrator. Words structure reality, as in dreams.[38] Social impotence means literally to shrink in size and progressively to fade away;[39] loss of speech is equated with loss of existence. Within the alien environment the migrant subjects progressively dissolve: from "tallest...in the world", to being confined in a house, then a room, a box, to hiding under the bed, to nothing ("the white snow that was nowhere"). Even names, potent signifiers of social identity, disappear (a common motif in migrant writing).

In "Poland"[40] the memory of the previous culture becomes rapidly transformed into a total fabrication: "child stories", stories told by a child and to a child. Again meaning is dependent on words organized at a literal level: memory, like a piece of cloth, fades and then disappears. Those who have gone "over the horizon line" have died. Initially, there is the link provided by dreams ("I went back every night") but when these are not confirmed by the daily life, the past place and the past self disappear. Poland becomes "Poland", simply a place on the map which one reads about in the papers.[41] Underlying the vehement tone of the poem is the harrowing implication that the self constructed over there has no currency in the present "here" and "now": a self which was introduced into and derived from a particular cluster of signifying systems becomes irrelevant here ("This is finished and finished...gone and is gone").

In "wogs"[42] the predicament is viewed, so to speak, from the other side. An unpunctuated, relentless chorus announces the stereotypes of prejudice familiar to immigrants. Although it is an evocation of untutored voices, full of contradictions, it reminds one uncannily of certain enunciations deriving from so-called high culture.[43] The logical momentum of the poem invokes all the standard fears associated with racism: miscegenation; alien food; skin the wrong colour; uncontrolled breeding. All add up to the concept of "wogs" as non-human ("dark skin monkeys"). The more recently published "europe"[44] is also based on stereotypic images from popular culture, in this case, the discourse of travelogues. The narrator, initially not gendered, catalogues European diversity metonymically and appropriately as consisting of rich food. There is also a hint of the pre-Oedipal and pre-linguisitic child who recognizes no boundaries and absorbs the world, everything, into its own body ("inside me is Europe"). As in post-war Australia, the signifier "Europe" gestures towards an undifferentiated conglomeration of foreign countries. Once again, as in the beginning of "Poland", there is the sense that living memory, the actual memory of Europe, displaces or is more palpable than the here and now of the new place. In this case though, the tone is more mocking and parodic, as though the readers were being served only with the concepts (if not the forms) they expected. The advent of "carl" fresh from Europe, shifts the narrator's "europe" back into dreams ("I ride in my first night with goblins"). The narrator labours to sustain and give back body to "europe" as reminiscence, but is increasingly dependent on the support of artifacts such as pictures. The reference to "soir de paris perfume my wrist" hints at gender, only to be displaced shortly after by, "I'm young man".[45] In this final mastery of "europe" the narrator is established as male, Teutonic and full of potential ("everything is going to be").

The final poem in Walwicz's first collection is titled "New World"[46] and is the paradoxical celebration of a subject who is visibly there but who refuses his own history. Beginning as "Mister New" with no forebears the narrator simultaneously refers to "prison" and to "hospital" thus signalling precisely the past which is being disavowed. Gender becomes increasingly complicated when Mister New gives birth to a new self ("I give me birth"). The male autogenesis is presumably more authoritative than the more familiar female parthenogenesis, but is then qualified by "Thin dress...Joy is my name".[47] For those who are marked negatively by social sign systems (migrant, female) the possibility of re-birth is a compelling fantasy. It is accompanied, explicitly and implicitly, by the concept of an autonomous and originating subject. This theme is celebrated at greater length in the poem "I"[48] ("I am the driver...I am the world. There is nothing outside of me"). Paradoxically, what is finally signalled here is that stage *before* the subject develops subjectivity: the period when the child cannot distinguish between itself and the world at large.

Focussing more clearly on the construction of gender in Walwicz's poetry it is useful to refer back to Juliet Mitchell's statement quoted above. If one recalls that the hysteric refuses to line up on one side or the other of a socially constituted sexual division, then Walwicz's poetry is indeed filled with this refusal. "Masculinity" and "femininity" are displayed as a series of poses and masquerades rather than referring to any essential truths.[49] For example, "The All Male Sauna" begins with, "I was a little girl again" which sets the tone for a tongue-in-cheek catalogue of "femininity" (what are little girls made of...). What is being celebrated here is the over-determined femininity which one associates with female impersonators but which is, at the same time, part of a continuum of what constitutes "normal" femininity in our own society.[50] Also on this continuum is the notion of the fetish, succinctly described by Elizabeth Wright as an over-investment in something in order to cover over a lack.[51] In "Photos"[52] the anxieties engendered by the fragmented, or even non-existent, self are covered over with fetishized images. The endless taking of photos becomes a guarantee of existence, serving to manufacture what Althusser has termed "interpellation"[53] - the recognition or hailing of the subject by social institutions ("So other people will look at me and see me"). Again there is the concept of autogenesis and self-control, or, control over the self. What gets recorded is of course not a unified self but a series of selves (and here the strip of photos on the book's cover becomes teasingly contextualised. The self exists only on film (or in writing), "This comes out of me" and is unified only through the assertions of the narrator's "I" ("I want to catch what I feel....This is really me"). But as we know from Benveniste [54] the signifier "I" has meaning only within the terms of the discourse in which it appears (for example, in relation to a "you") and not in relation to an outside referent. Thus the repetition in the poem of "I" perversely draws attention to the very absense that is being strenuously denied. The vehement affirmation of a unified subject puts that very concept into question.

Antigone Kefala has come to Australia via Rumania, Greece and New Zealand in the last of which she received her tertiary education. Her prose works clearly explore gender roles: *The First Journey* and *The Island* [55] in particular. Kefala's poetry, however, establishes a narrator who is not easily or consistently gendered but who clearly does derive from a "foreign" culture and so draws attention to a cultural double (or more) vision. The informing perspective is European rather than Australian, or New Zealand, though most of her poetry so far comments ostensibly on the last. As in the case of Walwicz's work dreams also play a significant role but in very different ways.

When one is deprived of a collective unconscious, in the sense of a shared body of mythic underpinnings, what does one have left but a recourse to personal dreams? Kefala inserts what often appear to be very personal and idiosyncratic dream sequences but this may be, more precisely, a strategy for constituting a new body of myth. In other words, what appears to be very personal is in fact a way of moving beyond the specific individual to that territory of the personal which everyone shares. In one sense the concept of the Jungian collective unconscious may be a misnomer. As Lacan would have it, the unconscious is always collective, that is social, and, moreover, functions like a language, also social. It may, therefore, be more accurate to speak of a mythic dimension (including the ritualisation of daily acts) which comprises a crucial element in that elusive concept we term culture. We all dream but not all cultures acknowledge the importance of circulating dreams as part of the daily, fully conscious life. If one is displaced to a part of the world where public dreaming (a mythic system) has quite different resonances, or none at all, what is left but to draw attention to this absence and to begin to fashion a new mythography.

> Dreaming allows for, supports, releases, brings to light an extreme delicacy of moral, sometimes even metaphysical, sentiments, the subtlest sense of human relations, refined differences, a learning of the highest civilization, in short a conscious logic, articulated with an extraordinary finesse, which only an intense waking labor would be able to achieve. In short, dreaming makes everything in me which is not strange, foreign, speak: the dream is an uncivil anecdote made up of very civilized sentiments (the dream is civilizing). [56]

In dreams begins the journey...

The first words of Kefala's earliest collection. Australian and New Zealand culture and myth are predicated upon journeys so that the chord touched here creates a group of readers who can indeed concur, at some level, that we are all immigrants. Immediately after this tenuously shared territory is established, there evolves a landscape utterly foreign to Anglo-Celtic readers:

> In dreams begins the journey, they would say
> moving the candle in the darkened room
> that smelt of cherry jam and basil.
> I watched their shadows moving on the walls
> straining to hear the corners creaking in the dark
> afraid of the black night that fell outside

in silent, feathered sheets, of the abandoned
courtyard, save for the big dogs,
and far away the well.[57]

Insofar as the cherry jam, basil, courtyard and well constitute a familiar foreignness it is a textual one that vaguely conjures a (possibly) Greek territory transmitted here via the nineteenth-century Romanticism of Byron or the twentieth-century romanticism of Lawrence Durrell. Those to whom it speaks with utter familiarity are Greek Australians (or Greek New Zealanders). The landscape evoked in the poem lacks distracting detail, as in old photos. The narrator recalls a childhood and a hidden menace of adult voices issuing from darkness with their prohibitions, hinting at the dead and the threats of the past. The escape, in the last stanza, attributed to the (posssibly) dead Katka. conjures a childhood land of Cockayne which dispels the dark:

....And you are the light, shadowless, falling
upon these fields forever petrified in silence.

These ambiguous last lines make it unclear whether it is the "fields" or the "you" which will be forever "petrified in silence". References to gender have intruded earlier linking women, the well, the darkness, "wild men's eyes" and again the notion of silence ("dumb mouths").

The gender of the narrator in "Memory"[58] is hinted at only through the introductory quotation from Sophocles' *Antigone*. Antigone, that proper name from Western myth, who puts family ties above duty to the State figures, not unexpectedly, in this poet's private pantheon. Here again, we are presented with the motif of being uprooted, this time in conjunction with the dutiful daughter who guards both father and brother. Antigone, daughter of Oedipus, shares his exile and after his apotheosis defies her uncle in order to bury her rebel brother.

The opening lines of the poem address the epigraph and signal the context of exile, both from country and from sustaining Gods (significantly, these are plural and capitalised for we are not on familiar Christian soil). The second stanza moves into a dream where a maternal "I" cradles for a "you" suffering from "some dark disease" - possibly the exile itself, or something more. Men in uniform converge silently. In the second part the "you" remains fitfully lost in the darkness but sometimes recaptures the "far country" of the past with its "stray sunray, some meaning..." The "you" is distinguished from an "us" who are protected by "narrow knowledge...and our social ways". The third section evokes a "common house" of locked doors and men in white.

'They steal my time', you said in a low voice.
Then watched the floor as if my presence were too much
And in the silence, the white men moved,
their pockets full of time, their steps so sure
cushioned by what they stole.
'They steal my time, I shall not last much longer.'
And I protested, unconvinced, for you had aged so much.
And who could say what they forced out of you

66

behind those walls. The essence maybe of our time,
dripping so slowly in our blood.
Maybe they stole the measure.

Like Oedipus's daughter this speaker too considers the possibility that
enlightenment may well emerge from those cast out of the familiar social context.
Oedipus the outcast did after all bestow the most powerful guiding myth of
Western civilization, though the nature of the guidance may still contain
unexplored interpretive possibilities.

The last line of the stanza quoted above re-echoes in the opening stanza of the
title poem of the second collection and offers one possible gloss on "measure".

To find our measure, exactly,
not the echo of other voices.
The present growing out of our lungs
like a flower, with a smell
that we have re-traced through our veins
some dark, secret smell
that will bloom when the hour has struck
an animal smell
reminiscent of blood
the world's scent.[59]

In this poem a "we" is established as firmly bonded by a communal experience of
"foreignness". The first part explores a disjunction between subjects and place; all
are reduced to shadows. The second part moves once again into the alternative
realities of madness. The "you" of "memory" echoes in, "They were stealing your
time...". The mark of madness settles silently, disguising blood as golden powder,
the inner nightmare still contained by the ordered daily self. Part three recalls the
dark room and disruptive "foreign laugh" of "memory" but fleshes out in further
detail the encroaching hallucinations which manifest themselves in "the silent
room". In the outside world the counterpoint hymn to Mary carries an
undercurrent of menace in its appellation "Siren of the Waters" and in its "chorus
of women, black clad". The "new" religion barely contains the old. Part four
follows the stricken emissary to the nightmare house which contains gorgons'
heads and the message, "The virgin they had hidden". The old forces appear to
have triumphed, though the nature of their victory is only hinted in -

...the mirrors everywhere
blooming relentlessly, pools of white fire
unable to contain the unimagined.

The final part offers images of "the ring" and menacing "nets" which evoke the
bloodthirsty world of the *Oresteia*, or even older orders. The "you" is enmeshed in
sacrificial rituals and the earlier allusions to light and fire culminate in the image
of "fire worshippers" and "thirsts no air could cure". The final stanza, akin to the
end of "Memory", observes the troubled "you" caught in an obsessive search for
water; the mechanised miming of actions which strips them of their usual
meanings and which one encounters in the dying and the insane.

67

The effect of the poem is of an intensely personal but completely private experience. The details bring it to vivid life but do not evoke specific individuals; we never even know the nature of the bond between the narrator and the protagonist. The movement at the end recalls the Freudian and Lacanian concept of aphanisis - the fading of the subject.[60] When the myths are withdrawn and social rituals no longer signify, when possible selves proliferate, there is a fear of inundation and of not emerging as a subject at all, or of not being able to sustain subjectivity. Most graphically this is rendered in the title poem "The Alien".[61] It surfaces also in the "Eumenides" section of "Farewell Party":

> my shape was going from me
> while I watched it.[62]

The Eumenides are the chthonic goddesses of (perhaps) a matriarchal era in which blood ties and the rights of the mother and of the earth dominated in law.

Kefala's poetry constructs a writing subject for whom the use of words is not a reassuring entry into the social but, rather, a journey on to a tight-rope with no safety nets.[63] It is a process, moreover, where visibility in the public world is too often confined to the execution of clever tricks (shades here of Walwicz's gender masquerades) and the loss of a darkness and silence which offer other, and perhaps shattering, possibilities.

The family constellation, so often a ghetto of solidarity in realist migrant writing,[64] is here breached and vulnerable and offers no protection.

> I am tired, living at home among strangers,
> sitting at the same tables,
> waiting for an acceptance that never comes,
> an understanding that would not be born,
> the measure in us already spent.[65]

The family group disperses into individuals isolated by their non-interpellation - they are not hailed into social identity. A much later poem on this theme is set within the context of a return to Europe but here too the family proffers no help:

> Marble dusted, ancient faces
> with eroded eyes,
> shell eyes of statues bleached by time.[66]

The eyes offer no reflection, no confirmation. One recalls that in Lacanian territory it is the terrain and gaze of the Other which consolidates the subject. The Other may consist of the social in many forms: the mother, language, a range of signifying systems.

While Kefala's novellae explore gender roles in some detail the poetry does so only sporadically. As in the case of Walwicz's work, gender roles are depicted as masks, costumes, charades. For example, "At the Pictures" offers a disturbing spectacle of the traditional young couple:

They had started the evening together,
waiting in their seats, the girl silent,
the boy noisy, with curly hair,
his busy hands touching her hungrily,
like a thirsty man who would never
have enough, eating her away, diligently,
absorbed, with vacant eyes.
The hunger not his, passed on,
untouched, from the beginning,
inhabiting shadows.[67]

The shadows contain the lurking gods who often inhabit the wings in Kefala's work and who enact in this example their traditional rites of possession. The comment on gender traditions is clear and devastating.

In "Concert" we have elderly women performing their allotted role as bearers of culture, "powdered white...suspended...in ether."[68] Pathetically anachronistic these votaries are, like their culture, slightly out of place. The final stanza, however, transfigures them and gives renewed significance to their own "promised land" and "unseen god". A different kind of elderly woman appears in "The Women in Black",[69] sustained by another kind of faith - Christian but linked also with older gods who inhabit other poems. Such figures (women in black) are rooted in the earth and are in touch with its chthonic powers. It may be that the later work will link more closely the "lady herself"[70] of the Christian pantheon, with other goddesses.

Goddess

The evening was falling
on the porcelain dust
that moved on the waters
the milky white breath
of the goddess with snakes
who travelled below
her slim arms outstretched
poised at the centre
a secretive smile
on her listening mouth.

At her feet
the octopus waited
watchful
with eyes of the deep.[71]

After all, others too have seen a connection between pre-Christian snake goddesses and the traditional icon of Mary standing on the serpent.

The two poems which conclude *Thirsty Weather* offer the convergence of a series of places from which the writing subject has been speaking in the course of both volumes. In "Epilogue",[72] there is a collective "we" moving like lost souls or Homeric shadows in the limbo of "long medicinal rooms". For non Anglo-Celtic readers whose voices are not yet acknowledged within mainstream Australian culture this is a poignant image. The fate of lurking insanity depicted in "Memory" and "Thirsty Weather" haunts all those who have been uprooted from the signifying systems which gave them positive meanings. In the final poem, "The Hour", a dreaming narrator witnesses the silent murder of another alien people, culturally identified by the reference to "greenstone tongues".[73] The image of Maori suffering is juxtaposed with Tiresias, the bisexual poet and seer who is then linked with the narrator.

Kefala is not the first non-Anglo-Celtic writer to seek affinity with other silenced voices. It is interesting to see how she taps the pre-white mythic darkness of New Zealand and links it with her own mythic legacy in order to construct, via dreams, a new language of myth. In this enterprise gender is not paramount, at least not so much in the poetry. Both individual and, at the same time, impersonal, Kefala's poetry constructs fragments of migrant subjects which draw the attention of some Australian readers to a "foreignness" with which they should be more familiar. To other Australians, aware of their hyphenated cultural affiliations, she signals "a new measure".

In a recent book *Criticism in the Wilderness*, the American critic Geoffrey Hartman has shown that the struggle for cultural definition is often accompanied by notions of purifying a national language. "Nation" becomes conflated into "natural" with attendant dangers of fascism:

> Any call for purification or repristination is dangerous. For it is always purity having to come to terms with impurity that drives crazy. The situation is familiar: and whatever the motive for purity, language and religion are its major battlegrounds. The language of religion especially: but also the religion of language itself. Language as a quasireligious object when a new vernacular is developing.[74]

One of the ways of removing the birthstain of Australia as the penal colony, a way of recreating a pre-lapsarian state, is to conjure up notions of a universal language arising spontaneously out of an interaction between the mother country and her children: Adam born of Adamah (Hebrew: the earth) and naming his world. But, as Hartman reminds us, this is a dangerous myth.

> What we get to see is always a palimpsest or a contaminated form of some kind: a stratum of legitimate, sacred, or exalted words purifying a stratum of guilty, forbidden, or debased words.[75]

In this case the forbidden, the prohibited, are the non Anglo-Celts who embody in themselves notions of contamination and the alien. Themselves displaced, they displace, place. That is to say they remind us of the arbitrary and manufactured nature of national identity, territory and language. Within their manifest struggles to speak we hear the trace of all the other "natural" languages jostling to produce reality. In their conspicuous reading of Australian culture they remind us that we are all taught to read this culture in specific and analysable ways.

Writing as a migrant woman, reading as a non-Anglo-Celtic woman is a way of marking the dominant term as gendered or encultured in particular ways. In other words, reading as a woman demands that reading as a man is merely another option and not the norm. Reading and writing as a migrant woman means that Anglo-Celtic Australian male or female is also no longer the norm.

Notes

1 A. Kefala, "Thirsty Weather", *Thirsty Weather*, Outback Press, Victoria, 1978, p.8.

2 W.H. Wilde et al., *The Oxford Companion to Australian Literature*, Oxford University Press, Melbourne, 1985.

3 L. Kramer (ed), *My Country: Australian Poetry and Short Stories*, Landsdowne Press, Sydney, 1985.

4 *Outrider: a journal of multicultural literature in Australia*, 2.2, December 1985, pp.60-61.

5 See the distinction made by J. Delaruelle in "Multiculturalism: a Walk in 'The Garden of the I Don't Know What'", *Writing in Multicultural Australia*, ed. J. Delaruelle and A. Karakostas-Seda, Australia Council, Sydney, 1985, p.51.

6 For more details see S. Gunew, "Australia 1984: A Moment in the Archaeology of Multiculturalism", *Europe and its others*, v.i. ed. F. Barker et al., University of Essex, Colchester, 1985, pp.178-193.

7 T. Eagleton, *Literary Theory: An Introduction*, Blackwell, Oxford, 1983, p.209.

8 S. Gunew, "Multicultural Writers: Where are We Writing From and Who Are We Writing For?", *Writing in Multicultureal Australia*, op. cit., pp.15-23.

9 S. Gunew, "Denaturalizing Cultural Nationalisms: Multicultural Readings of 'Australia'" (forthcoming).

10 As traced in general terms in B. Anderson, *Imagined Communities*, Verso, London, 1983.

11 T. Eagleton, "The Subject of Literature", *Cultural Critique*, 2 (1986), p.98.

12 A reference to the notion of a public and counterpublic sphere developed in T. Eagleton, *The Function of Criticism*, Verso, London, 1984.

13 S. Gunew, "Migrant Women Writers: Who's on Whose Margins?", *Gender, Politics and Fiction*, ed. C. Ferrier, University of Queensland Press, 1985.

14 For Example, see S. Gunew, "Multicultural Reading Strategies: Cappiello's *Oh Lucky Country* ", *Meanjin*, 44.4 (1985), 517-528.

15 R. Cappiello, *Oh lucky country*, University of Queensland Press, St. Lucia, 1984. For extracts, see appendix.

16 M. Bakhtin, *Rabelais and His World*, M.I.T. Press, Cambridge, Massachusetts, 1968, p.317.

17 U. Loewald, "Silver Jubilee", *Difference*, op. cit., pp.16-18. See appendix.

18 G.L. Ulmer, "The Object of Post-Criticism", *Postmodern Culture* , ed. H. Foster, Pluto Press, London, 1983, p.95.

19 R. Barthes, *Writing Degree Zero*, Cape, London, 1967, p.38.

20 Ibid., p.25

21 Ibid., p.48

22 S. Gunew, "Migrant Women Writers", op.cit.

23 Defined by Anthony Wilden as "the order of discursive and symbolic action", *The Language of the Self*, Johns Hopkins University Press, Baltimore, 1968, p.xii.

24 See K. Silverman, *The Subject of Semiotics*, Oxford University Press, N.Y., 1983, Ch.2.

25 Ibid., p. 67. "A drive provides a psychic mediation and expression of a physiological phenomenon". In other words, it is not to be confused with the instincts.

26 Ibid., p.176.

27 T. Eagleton, *Literary Theory: An Introduction*, Blackwell, Oxford, 1983, pp.169-170.

28 "Benveniste's writings suggest that even from the most 'orthodox' of semiotic perspectives - the linguistic - the sign cannot be detached from discourse, discourse from the subject, or the subject from the symbolic order. Language can only be studied through the concrete signifying formations within which it manifests itself, formations which implicate the subject as signifier, as product of the discourse. Moreover, language, discourse, and subject must all be understood as determined by the particular symbolic order within which they emerge." Silverman, op.cit., p.53.

29 See, for example, *Aboriginal Writing Today*, ed. J. Davis and B. Hodge, Australian Institute of Aboriginal Studies, Canberra, 1985, and *Reading the Country*, K. Benterrak, S. Muecke, P. Roe, et al., Fremantle Arts Centre Press, Fremantle, 1984.

30 For example, D. Modjeska, *Exiles At Home*, Sirius, London, Sydney, 1981, and *Gender, Politics and Fiction*, op.cit.

31 That naturalization still represents an important rite of passage within Australian culture is shown by the fact that Victoria's recently appointed Governor-elect hastily went through the process although he had lived here for many decades

32 See, for example, C.O. Ogunyemi, "Womanism: the dynamics of the contemporary black female novel in English", *Signs*, 11.1, Autumn 1985, pp.63-80.

33 J. Mitchell, *Women: the Longest Revolution*, Virago, London, 1984, pp.289-290. If one were re-writing this passage in terms of culture (rather than gender) one might consider substituting "multiculturalism" for "bisexuality".

34 One thinks here of Habermas's concept of ideal speech acts which are based on the assumption that consensus is possible. I am indebted for this reference to Dr. I. Veit-Brause.

35 Walwicz's performance ability can be sampled in the record included with the recent anthology *Off the Record*, ed. Pi.O., Penguin, Ringwood, Victoria, 1985.

36 "Displacement involves the transfer of psychic intensity from an unacceptable element to an acceptable one, while condensation effects the formation of a new signifier from a cluster of previous signifying materials. In other words, the first of these agencies neutralizes the differences between two similar or continguous things by asserting their emotional equivalence, while the second achieves the same thing by insisting on their absolute coincidence". Silverman, op.cit., p.89.

37 A. Walwicz, "So Little", *Mattoid*, 13, University of Deakin, p.19, See also "helpless" in *Displacements: Migrant Story-tellers*, ed. S. Gunew, University of Deakin Press, 1982, p.2 and "so small", *Narrative Unit B Reader*, Deakin University Press, 1982, p.15.

38 "Freud observes that it is characteristic of the primary process to treat words as if they were things, with all the same affective and sensory properties". Silverman, op.cit., p.84.

39 I am thinking here of "aphanisis" (the fading of the subject). See J. Lacan, *The Four Fundamental Concepts of Psychoanalysis*, Penguin, Harmondsworth, 1977, pp.216-229 and J. Lacan, *Ecrits*, Tavistock, London, 1977, pp.283-284.

40 A. Walwicz, *Writing*, Rigmarole Press, Melbourne, 1982, p.37.

41 Poland functions as the "lost object" of psychoanalysis: "The erotogenic zones or somatic gaps become the points through which the child attempts to introject into itself those things which give it pleasure, and which it does not yet distinguish from itself. The first such object is generally the breast, and it is of course inserted into the orifice of the mouth. ...Other objects which enjoy the same privileged status are the feces, and the gaze and voice of another, such as the mother.

There will be many such objects in the life of the subject. Lacan refers to them as "objets petit a", which is an abbreviation for the more complete formula "objets petit autre".

This rubric designates objects which are not clearly distinguished from the self and which are not fully grasped as other (autre). The object derives its value from its identification with some missing component of the subject's self, whether that loss is seen as primordial, as the result of a bodily organisation, or as the consequence of some other division", Silverman, op.cit., p.156.

42 Walwicz, "wogs", *Mattoid*, op.cit., pp.16-17.

43 One thinks here of the figurative underpinnings of G. Blainey's *All for Australia*, Methuen Haynes, Sydney, 1984.

44 A. Walwicz, "Europe", *Joseph's Coat: An Anthology of Multicultural Writing*, ed. P. Skrzynecki, Hale and Iremonger, Sydney, 1985, pp.195-6.

45 One thinks of the identification with an ideal self marked by the mirror stage in the Lacanian model. See Silverman, op.cit., p.158.

46 Walwicz, *Writing*, op.cit., p.67.

47 It may be appropriate to recall Blake's "Infant joy" and "Infant sorrow" here.

48 Walwicz, "I", *Mattoid*, op.cit., p.22.

49 See, for example, C. Owen, "Posing", *Difference: On Represenation and Sexuality*, The New Museum of Contemporary Art, New York, 1985, pp.7-18.

50 Walwicz has many poems dealing with bisexuality in the collection *Writing*. See also her recent contribution to *Girl/boy talk* performed at the Anthill Theatre, Melbourne, January 1985

51 E. Wright, *Psychoanalytic Criticism*, Methuen, London, 1984, p.93. See also Ch. 5, Silverman, op.cit.

52 Walwicz, *Writing*, op.cit., p.56.

53 L. Althusser, *Essays on Ideology*, Verso, London, 1976, p.44 ff.

54 Referred to in Silverman, op.cit., pp.185-186.

55 A. Kefala, *The First Journey*, Wild Woolley, Sydney, 1975 and *The Island*, Hale & Iremonger, Sydney, 1984.

56 R. Barthes, *The Pleasure of the Text*, Hill & Wang, N.Y., 1975,pp.59-60. I am indebted to Judy Brett for alerting me to the prevalence of dreams in Kefala's work. See J. Brett, "The Process of Becoming": Antigone Kefala's *The First Journey* and *The Island*, *Meanjin*, 44.1, March 1985, pp.125-133.

57 A. Kefala, "Holidays in the Country", *The Alien*, Makar, St. Lucia, 1973, p.5.

58 A. Kefala, "Memory", *The Alien*, op.cit., p.17.

59 A. Kefala, "Thirsty Weather", op.cit.

60 Refer back to footnote 39.

61 "The Alien", *The Alien*, op.cit., p.20.

62 "Farewell Party", *Thirsty Weather*, op.cit., p.42.

63 See A. Kefala, "The Acrobat", *The Alien*, op.cit., p.11.

64 Some of the finest writing in this mode are the two autobiographal novels produced by Maria Lewitt: *Come Spring*, Scribe, Fitzroy, 1980 and *No snow in December*, Heinemann, Melbourne, 1985.

65 A. Kefala, "Family Life", *The Alien*, op.cit., p.8.

66 A. Kefala, "Family", *Meanjin*, 42.1, March 1983, p.29.

67 A. Kefala. "At the Pictures", *The Alien*, op.cit., p.16.

68 A. Kefala, "Concert", *The Alien*, op.cit., p.9. For related presentations of women "acting out" a certain kind of "femininity", see also "Deserted Wife" and "Old Friend", both in *Thirsty Weather*, op.cit.

69 A. Kefala, "The Woman in Black", *Thirsty Weather*, op.cit., p.22.

70 A. Kefala, "Parish Church", *Meanjin*, 42.1, March 1983, p. 28.

71 A. Kefala, "Goddess", *Meanjin*, 44.1, March 1985, p.61.

72 A. Kefala, "Epilogue", *Thirsty Weather*. op.cit., p.52.

73 A. Kefala, "The Hour", *Thirsty Weather*, op.cit., p.53.

Antigone Kefala. Photo: James Murdoch.

Towards a Language

Antigone Kefala

"Who can refuse to live one's own life?"
                    Anna Akhmatova

I was born and spent my childhood in Romania, in a small city on the Danube called Braila. A city, according to my Mother, with some cultural aspirations, that had seen Eleonora Duse in Ibsen, and in which writers such as Panait Istrati had been born and lived.

The family was mostly Greek, on both sides, and had been in Braila for some generations. On Father's side, they had come from Messolonghi and Asia Minor, on Mother's side, from Ithaca.

A number of languages were spoken at home. Father had been educated at a French school, taught Greek at home and in schools, as well as Romanian. Mother learnt Greek when she married, in a household in which the grandparents spoke Greek. And my brother attended both Romanian and Greek schools, as well as studying German. In Romania at that time, as I think in most parts of Europe, a second or third language was considered an intrinsic part of one's education something that could only enhance one's understanding of other cultures, and provide direct access to valuable intellectual resources.

Both my Father and brother were musicians. Books, theatre, concerts, music at home were normal part of everyday living, as well as an attitude that evaluated the arts and considered them an essential and fundamental part of life. Artists were 'the heroes', so to speak, in spite of the dangers and the difficulties attached to their lives, and an everyday struggle that was known to us all through immediate experience.

Mother was the reader. She was full of an avid curiosity about the world, and read extensively. She had begun reading newspapers when she was ten, and continued to do so through four countries and two new languages. She was interested in politics, history and above all literature. Romania in spite of its size

A formal photograph of Antigone Kefala taken before the family left Romania.

Antigone Kefala's father and brother Homer - in the camp at Lavrion, near Athens. Photo taken by American photographer for IRO publicity purposes.

Antigone Kefala's family before she was born, her mother Anastasia, her father Kimon, and her brother Homer.

and resources, translated and published a large amount of literature from all European countries, America and Asia. Intellectual Romania was pro French, so we grew up with French literature.

It was difficult to imagine a musical career at home, or the space in which to pursue it. Someone was playing or practising at home most hours of the day, a thing that posed problems with neighbours, and forced the family to move from time to time.

I made some vague attempts to learn the piano, and for a while wanted to be an actor, but in the meantime I was "scribbling", as the family referred to it, complaining that the house was full of my papers. What I was scribbling I don't remember. When we left Romania everything was left behind. Two incidents related to writing have remained with me as fundamental experiences. The first is of an afternoon, when I must have been eleven or twelve. I was alone at home, in winter, I had just written something about the snow. I remember the warm room, the round walnut table on which I was working, the snow outside, and an immense inner excitement, as that of a craftsperson that has managed to solve the problem of the material and bring something off.

The second memory is connected with reciting, at primary school, a poem by the Romanian/French poet Elena Văcărescu, called "Ancestors". I don't remember the poem, what has remained in me was the magic by which the poem created spaces and states unknown before, making it possible to grasp realities far beyond my understanding at the time. The colour of the poem was sombre, struggling, a cave that took you in and brought you out in some open, magical field.

Then we left. For the family a difficult and slow decision, postponed in the hope of political change, and then the rush for visas, becoming for the first time part of a large group of people that were also trying to escape.

In Greece all my energies went into learning the language, going to school, passing examinations, everyone struggling in the same way, my brother at the Athens Conservatorium, Father trying desperately to find a job, Mother too. Living in camps maintained by the International Refugees Organization, all of us defined for the first time as "refugees", a definition and a position that would remain with us.

Suddenly everything in our lives reduced to the most simple elements, unplaced in a country that belonged to other people, a lack of knowledge or intimacy with the landscape, a disconnection in ourselves with what we had been or experienced before, a cut.

The change had a profound effect on the family, on its structure, it broke the unity as we had known it in Romania, each one was thrown out of the group, made to rely much more on their own resources. The struggle underlined both one's intrinsic vulnerability, as well as the family's inability to offer much support, and re-arrange the world for us. Not that it had been able to do this in Romania, but there it had not been asked by circumstances to prove it. The change affected deeply the relationship between my parents.

I learnt the language fairly quickly - we were in Greece for only three and a half years. I did not do much writing, and the few things I wrote were in Romanian, the language I still felt close to. In retrospect, even though by the time we reached Greece, I already knew Romanian, and some French, Greek surprised me enormously as a language, by its finesse, resonances which constantly brought into play a past intimately connected to philosophical, metaphysical issues. I remember reading a book on Plato that belonged to my brother, and finding suddenly that close relationship between the ideas expressed and their own natural language. It seemed to me then and now, that the landscape, the light, coloured constantly the language and one's understanding of the ideas, and that the essence was one of ease, that is even though a passionate, arguing, sometimes stubborn tone, intrinsically the approach of Greek was one that accepted itself in that position as a natural one, as if thinking, arguing, being passionately involved with life was a natural and accepted element.

What I also found interesting were the roots of the words, and the discovery of how interconnected a language is to a way of life, moral, social, and aesthetic assumptions. I remember the surprise in discovering that "areti", the word in Greek for virtue, came from an ancient verb "ararisko", which meant to adjust, while the Latin derivation came from "vir", man. Obvious differences between the Greeks and the Romans.

Still, the family found it difficult to survive in Greece. At the time of our arrival, at the end of 1947, the country was full of the devastation of the war. Then the Civil War started. And as refugees seem to suffer generally from the same recurrent idea - how to escape - the family began applying again to emigrate. Emigration at any rate was in the air in Europe. Then followed long interviews to prove our suitability, commissions, medical check-ups, and suddenly we discovered that what they wanted from us, "a perfect medical record", was outside our possibilities. Mother was found to have a small shadow on one lung.

This shadow caused enormous difficulties. A constant postponement, the necessity for Mother to go into hospital for prolonged check-ups and observation, until finally and miraculously (even though she had been cleared, Australia did not want to take us), New Zealand accepted for the first time a boatload of Southern European refugees, and we were on our way to New Zealand.

The most direct and dramatic impact of New Zealand was the climate, and the fact that the country was so green, so totally, so permanently green, at the beginning and after Greece, a very fanciful colour that meant good things.

So we started all over again, less equipped than in Greece, totally lost now because of our lack of language and understanding of New Zealand life and attitudes. Constantly undermined by this cattle-like approach, we were mustered in groups, defined in groups as a special category, unable to be part of anything in a normal way, made to feel that our faces, our gestures, belonged to this outside category with which the locals did not want to become involved.

We immediately set to learn the language. We had made a beginning in Greece, and in the camp at Pahiatua, we did a six month course in English that equipped most people before they were sent to work or school.

But the difficulties continued afterwards, in this slow intimate process related to the total changes in our life. A changed everyday that automatically imposed a new framework on any analysis we might do, and for which we still did not have the analytical tools. The basic assumptions of a language come out of a way of life, a past history, cultural and moral norms. The language of our past was of little use here, and the one belonging to the country we did not possess.

At the beginning I was too stunned to do anything. Some sort of inner "dyslexia". I was running between Romanian, Greek and now English. Where could one find a basis for anything? How was one to view things? All these combined with long and great difficulties, including major illness in the family.

Still we went on learning, reading. Mother took up her newspapers and books in English, Father his music. I struggled at the University taking subjects that might help me pass - French, Greek.

At home we thought, we spoke, we analysed constantly, going back and forth, working all these happenings, trying to make some sense of them, place them in some form. Listening to life around us, trying to understand it, the people. We had been conditioned since Romania to understand life, a country by its art forms. We were desperate to find New Zealand writers, painters, composers, thinkers. How did they find things? What was their analysis, their image of the country? But these were difficult to find in New Zealand in the fifties. It was as if the country had no past, no voice, everything pointed to Britain. Yet the landscape, the Maoris, the Maori wars, all implied a locality that was disconnected from Britain.

Antigone Kefala. Photo by Penny Tweedie.

At University and elsewhere, because I did my degree mostly on a part time basis, while holding jobs, I looked avidly for interesting people, or oddities like us. Slowly I began to set down a few primitive impressions of life around me. The most positive gesture that I made towards a serious commitment to writing, was to buy in instalments a small, portable typewriter. This was in December 1955.

Still for a long time I could not find a language, or a style that would release any of the things inside. In my last years at the university I began writing short stories and for the first time found the courage to submit them and was amazed that a few were published. Two in a university magazine, and one in Auckland. This was in 1959.

And as I finished the university, as unsolvable events in my life were mounting, I left for Australia.

AUSTRALIA...AUSTRALIA... we entered Sydney harbour a summer morning. The colours of the rock wall at The Gap were warm apricot, the sun was coming down on the waters, the whole landscape shimmering, overflowing with light, with heat, with movement.

I was suddenly released from the greenness, from the rain, the wind, released, at least for the moment, from my inner problems. My past in Romania, in Greece came back as a meaningful experience in a landscape that had similar resonances. Sydney seemed alive with people, activity and intellectual excitement.

When I arrived in December 1959, Australia, it seemed to me, was very interested in discovering itself. Books about Australia were everywhere. I felt that I too could take part in this. The landscape was already feeling familiar, allowing me to survive, the landscape was more at ease with itself, more generous in its attitude. Indifferent maybe, but on a large scale, the very scale allowed for more imaginative potential.

For the first time I began to write as an on going, everyday activity. I wrote in the Mitchell Library after work. Typed things out at weekends, surprised myself that I had finally found a voice, at the beginning terribly pleased with my own voice, with a feeling of levitation, of having escaped the constraints of gravity. The climate, the landscape, my own inner release coincided to give me a feeling of euphoria.

I began to submit a few things and some were accepted, and then to give credence to my optimism, a novella I had sent to the Adelaide Advertiser's Competition, won a special prize. Telegrams were coming from publishers, from friends, from the family who was still in New Zealand. Ian Mudie, working at the time with Jacaranda Press was very taken with the novella and tried for many years to have it published. In spite of the youthfulness of the work, he wrote a very sensitive and warm report about it. P.R. Stephensen, Publisher's Editor and Authors' Agent, wrote offering his services.

For a brief period it was too good to be true. But slowly nothing happened. In spite of Ian Mudie's efforts, the novella never found a publisher. Except for Australian Letters, Hemisphere, and the ABC's "A First Hearing", all poems began to be rejected one by one, by all major and small magazines. I submitted them and they were returned. A good year meant two or three poems published.

The editorial comments, when they came, all hinted vaguely at the artificiality of my language, its exaggerated tone, an English with which they could not identify in linguistic or any other terms. An impression that the issues which preoccupied me, which seemed of importance were totally outside local preoccupations, both in approach and essence.

Almost my only support at that time and for many years, was my Mother, who read constantly what I was writing, with whom we had interminable discussions about the past, the present, our problems, literature, aesthetics....She had an unerring sense of style, but was very careful and not destructive in her criticism. I think that this was what sustained me for a long time, a respect for her ability to appraise literature, and the sense that she liked and respected what I wrote.

The turning point came with the seventies. Rodney Hall's poetry editorship of The Australian, Edward Kynaston's literary editorship of Nation Review, finally the Whitlam era, the renaissance of the small presses, the setting up of the Australia Council for the Arts, publishing subsidies, which allowed a generation of unpublishable (in commercial terms) writers to appear. A new spirit that gave evaluation to the mind, to intellectual activities, to the arts, to a re-appraisal, re-evaluation of Australia, of life here, connecting it to larger themes, to the outside world, to a spirit of curiosity. To the sudden impression that most things were possible in a matrix of life that had become more inclusive.

All this a short-lived illusion, to be swamped by conservative forces again, but which imaginatively showed what things could be achieved and that the possibilities were here.

I am asked whether I consider myself a migrant writer or an Australian writer. I can only say that I am both, and that the positions are not mutually exclusive.

The paradoxes under which a writer like myself works are two-fold - on the one hand, to express a difference in either tone, assumptions or approach, leads to constant rejections, and isolates one from a community of writers and readers, that place where people who are interested, labour all the time to re-define their cultural reality. On the other hand, the impossibility to absorb so rapidly, or take in wholesale the local colouring, because at the level at which a writer is working, one is dealing with forces that absorb very slowly, take years to change that transformation into an evaluation, a language, a style.

So while on the one hand, society resents the migrant's intrusion into its (assumed) safe, familiar world, on the other hand it would like to, or confesses to wanting to absorb the migrant totally, making him/her the same. Under what conditions would this total absorption take place? No one is certain, but what is constantly assumed is that such a transformation is simple, immediate and possible, and that it is the migrant's fault if it does not take place.

Still there are signs, especially with the presence now of a new generation born here, which belongs automatically and naturally to two cultures, that of their parents and of Australia, that the cultural oversimplifications that have plagued us, are slowly moving away, that the time may come when the recognition of a different kind of past, would not be a threat, and when all our memories and pasts can play an important role in the development of a culture in Australia and towards an understanding of the landscape in which we live.

The Wanderer

Antigone Kefala

The river
moved further away
in the heat of the road
shimmers of water
towards the horizon.

The salt
which they gave him at home
he would place on his tongue
to taste his own roots
and draw comfort.

The world
made of a matter that never
forgets, a symmetry so exact,
fatality at the heart
of each thing.

Australia - the Early Sixties. Drawing by Srebrenka Kunek.

ANIA WALWICZ
WRITING

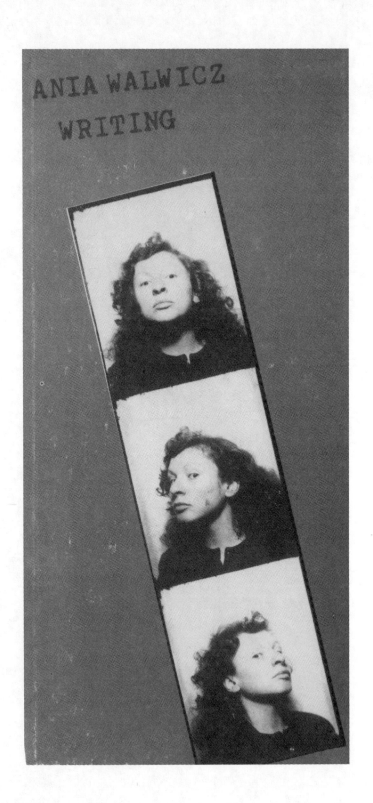

A Statement

Ania Walwicz

I was born in Poland in 1951 and came to Australia in 1963. I completed my secondary education in Australia and then studied at the Victorian College of Arts, School of Art.

I began to write in 1979. The work arose from diary writing, a record of the self. I began with the poetry form, which then developed into a prose/poetry format, with a growing abstraction of language and the loss of punctuation.

My writing, at first, had a literal, confessional tone and then I dealt with experience in a more general way. I became interested in the various levels and textures of language.

The aim of my work is the notation and enactment of inner states of feeling/being. I aim to write a record of my own experience which can be received and appropriated by others. I wish to directly convey experience using an appropriate form of language which enacts a particular state of feeling.

I am interested in the record of the present state and in the recollection of past experience. I aim to return, through language, to my own past experience and to the language of childhood.

I have an interest in experimental writing, in the sound formation of language and in capturing the immediacy of experience through language.

My first book, *Writing*, a collection of prose/poetry pieces, was published by Rigmarole Books, Melbourne in 1982. Since then, I have completed a second book of prose/poetry, *boat*. I have also written a play, "Girltalk and head master", excerpts from which formed the major part of "boygirltalk", Anthill Theatre, Melbourne 1986.

I am also interested in vocal performance. A tape-recording of my work, "Voice Performance of Prose/Poetry Text", was released by the Experimental Art Foundation in 1986.

no speak

Ania Walwicz

i no speak english sorry i where is john street where it is where please ticket and sixpence name what is dog what is house mary has a dog and a house has what pencil is this is a pencil good morning good morning what is pencil is my name is this is a book is a book my name is anne teacher is school is what is your name what time nine o'clock is time is what time is it please hello this is my bag this is lunch one o'clock what is your name my name is anne no speak sorry where is john street ticket bus mary dog mary has a dog mary has a house we go to school i don't speak no speak sorry my name is where is john street is please what is this this is a book this is a bus this is a house good morning hello my name is anne this is school this is teacher is this is lunch it is one o'clock mary has dog has bus has ticket is sixpence mary has house i no speak mary has a dog i no speak my name is anne this is school is nine o'clock is dog is my name is anne where john street is please ticket sixpence house is school is my name dog is this is a book this is a pencil this is teacher this school one o'clock good morning i no speak i no this teacher lunch time is book mary has a house is i no speak sorry i this where is john street please a ticket and a sixpence please i no speak where john street is where this is book this is school this is teacher this mary has a house i no speak sorry i this is a book what time three o'clock this is my bag this is lunchtime where is john is street is dog is john street mary has a house i no speak i no speak mary has a dog mary has a house i no speak mary has a dog i no speak mary has a house i no speak mary has i no ticket and sixpence this is my bag this is a bus this school is teacher is this school teacher anne mary dog house book pencil good morning good morning hello sorry i no speak this lunch one o'clock school mary has a house i no speak i no i no speak school teacher i no speak my name is what my name is anne i no speak i no speak mary has i no i no i no i no speak mary has mary has mary has a house i no speak mary has a dog i no speak mary has i no i no bus bus ticket sixpence sorry sorry sorry please i no i no i no speak mary has a book this is a book i no speak i no speak mary has i no i no speak mary has i no speak i no speak i no speak this book this teacher this what time where is john street please where john street is where john street is where it is where john street please sorry i no speak no speak this pencil is teacher is school good morning my name is anne i no speak i no speak this pencil mary has i no speak bus bus ticket and sixpence please mary has a house i no speak mary has i no mary has a dog i no speak this is my bag this is my bag this is my bag this is a dog this is a dog is this is a dog mary has school i no speak i no speak mary has mary has mary has teacher has teacher has i no speak i no speak where john street is where john street is i where is my name is anne where is john street bus bus ticket and sixpence i no speak what time is three o'clock i no speak i no speak i no speak this pencil teacher school this is lunch time i no speak i no speak i no speak this school is teacher is mary is i no i no speak i no speak i no speak mary has i no school is teacheris mary is i no i no speak i no speak i no speak mary has i no teacher has i no sorry sorry please i no speak where is where is where is john street is where john street is i no speak i no speak where it is john street is where is where is john street is where is john street where is i no speak teacher teacher i no speak mary has a dog mary has a house i no sorry i no i no teacher school pencil bag i no speak sorry we go to school we go to school good morning good morning bus ticket and sixpence is this is a bus this is my bag this is school this is hello this is good morning is i no speak i no speak this is lunch one o'clock i no speak i no speak this is school this teacher book pencil dog my name anne i no speak i no speak.

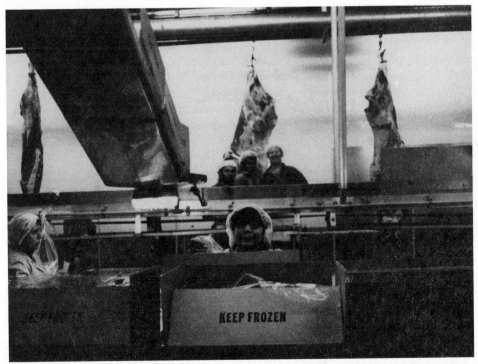

Mercy Knight - Indian migrant meat factory worker. Photo: Vivienne Mehes.

New World

I'm newborn. I'm new. Brand new. New. Me. I'm new. It doesn't matter what happened before. Now I'm new. I'm going to start a new life. Go to a new state. Make a clean. Break. With my past. To start afresh. Be new. I'm new. Mister New is my name. I'm new. I want to do new. What nobody else before. I get a new life. New bread. Crisp. I'm at the start of things. Right at the beginning. Right now. I don't think about anything. But now. I'm right here. At the beginning. I'm bright new and early. I'm first mark on my page. I get just born. I'm new here. I do my first year. I'm first spring. I'm dawn light. I'm early morning. I leave my hospital behind. I just get out of prison. I meet different people. Mister New is my name. I'm new. I get new clothes for my new life. I live now. I live now. I'm alive now. Yesterday I was heavy with me. And today I give birth. I give me birth. I give birth to myself. I'm shaky leg young horse. The afterbirth hangs from my back. Thin dress. I'm just new here. Joy is my name. I'm one day one. I'm here just new. I get just born. I'm a new girl. They ask me. Are you new around here? Are you new? And I say yes. I'm new. I don't know quite what to do but I'll learn. I'm new baby born. I do my first shout. I go to first grade. I'm new. I'm new. I'm new I'm first time first. I'm just here new. I don't want my past. I'm new. I've just made myself. I start just right. I'm new. I'm on the start line. Now. I'm new. I'm new. I'm new. Everything's different. From before. I'm new day new. I'm somewhere else than I was. I get this just here born fresh fresh. I'm early start. New day street. I'm clean clothes. I begin my piece. I do me right from the very start. I make myself anew. New. New. Everything's clear. And sharp

IF LIFE is something THEN IT MUST be IN SOMETHING

Photo: Peter Lyssiotis.

past

grandfather dances all men in a circle put arms around black coats white stockings shoes silver buckles ringlets black hat whirl fast faster to see godmother crawls through a hole to have a look twirl dervish poor merchant can't read or write other grandfather in post office of austro - hungarian empire lemberg puts wax in his moustache twirls it up comes home late and rings father sleeps in deep can't wake can't hear me grandfather sleeps on green baize cover of his post office desk joins austrian army grandfather puts on leggings to be a soldier fit all tight round and around my feet foot soldier goiter iodine on his shirt sweats burns up has to eat lots grandmother buys head of beef to make soup auntie mania aunt lola dies no money for grave father studies vet governor of galicia count gives him work father studies upstairs flat out window next to convent barefoot carmelites sleep in coffins beat whips father watches must study hard to examine cow doctorate in clotting of blood in dogs sits at dinner with count great grandfather brewer hops beer great great grandfather manager of estate great great great grandfather farmer i wear fat nose of grandfather in post office of austro-hungarian empire father saves money to go to paris war breaks out he escapes to russia put him in russian army shave all his hair grandfather dances to worship uncle boxer punches aunt in fire burns her face mother's mother dies wicked stepmother grandfather dances can't read or write ten children poor no roads lots of mud lublin never saw a car before makes her scream with fear germans come to kill with leggings tied mother translator first husband lawyer rosenberg skis and plays piano they catch him and they kill him father arranges to get married money no value take grandfather's pay home in a box he gets millions of marks isn't worth any at all grandfather sings and dances god watches they get killed and they all die i go to church and i pray where is he grandfather dances his black coat ringlets hat white stockings shoes silver buckles grandfather in austrian army marches father in russian army walks to berlin steals a painting and a lot of silk ties mother works in german office and hides builders bricklayers name is walwitz parents born in ussr on passports shift borders grandfather dances on saturday in his outfits father sleeps with his machine gun in a cold barn soldiers sleep in orphanage so tired big men sleep in baby cots their legs hang out they get killed and they die and i can't see them name singer werk grandfather dances salt herring in his barrel i put my trust in saint anthony holds baby jesus hangs above my bed germans come and kill him bauman half wit last nazi in town helps my mother in her orchard he looks after my baby sister gives her his boot to play with i wear polish national costume bunch of ribbons tied on my shoulder fly away on first of may i forgive everybody my best friend ewa schwidernoch grandfather in austrian army half wit bauman nazi grandfather god at night dance in a circle father in russian army marches to berlin to kill them all they sing songs and very jolly i fall in love with paul deutchmann kozminski count visits lives in an attic what is your name anna you have to hold your tongue against your mouth top for nnn i have to explain to grandfather can't write so he dances to worship i go faster now grandfather dances we move faster and faster in a circle around and around.

Wogs

They're not us they're them they're them they are else what you don't know what you don't know what they think they got their own ways they stick together you don't know what they're up to you never know with them you just don't know with them no we didn't ask them to come here they come and they come there is enough people here already now they crowd us wogs they give me winter colds they take my jobs they take us they use us they come here to make their money then they go away they take us they rip us off landlords they rise rent they take us they work too hard they take us they use us bosses we work in their factory rich wogs in wog cars rich jews in rich cars they take us they work so hard we are relaxed they get too much they own us they take my jobs away from me wogs they don't look like you or me they look strange they are strange they don't belong here they are different different skin colour hair they just don't look right they take us they land on us there isn't enough space for us now they come they work for less they can work in worse they take anything they work too hard they want from us we have to look after our own here not them let them go back where they come from to their own they're everywhere they get everywhere you can't speak to them why don't you learn to speak english properly they are not like you or me they're not the same as everybody they change us is your child educated by an australian? is it? do you know if? you don't know what they think you don't know what they can do here they change us they paint their houses blue green have you seen blue houses who ever heard of that they live too many together they're too noisy they chatter you don't know what they say they smell funny there's something funny about them strange not like you or me i don't want to see asian tram conductors they are not us not us they're them they're else what you don't know them nobody knows them they stick together they look after one another they don't care about us they're everywhere they're everywhere every day there's more of them we work in their factories they escape here we don't have to take them in this is our home they come we didn't ask them they spoil us they take us for what they can get they're not like us they behave different they're rude they act if they own the place they look wrong too dark too squat too short all wrong ugly too fat women go to fat dark skin monkeys i want to be with my own kind people like me exactly like me they stick out you can't miss them they're everywhere they shout they're noisy they're dirty they put vegetables in their front gardens they eat garlic they shouldn't have come here in the first place they're strangers i want to be with my own kind with my brothers with people like i am there's too many of them here already you don't know how to talk to them they're not clean they annoy me funny names luigi they got their own ways they don't do as you do they're aliens they look wrong they use us they take us they take us for what they can get from us then they go away they're greedy they take our space they not us not our kind they after what they can get they stick together i don't know what they say they don't fit in they dress wrong flashy they don't know our ways they breed and breed they take what little we got what is ours what belongs to us they take ours and ours they're not us

Family from Turkey. Migrated 1960's. Eldest son was born in Turkey. Daughter and youngest son born in Australia. Photo Angela Lynkushka.

What's in the Name?

S. Kucharova

The glass partitions between the individual offices provided Eve with a view on to the roofs and the walls of other high rise buildings and even some tree tops at a distance.

"It must be still too early for the afternoon tea" she thought, seeing very little movement emerging from the other rooms. She stretched her legs and decided to sift through the conference paper which arrived in the morning mail. While she was fully absorbed in the paper the phone rang. It rang a couple of times before she reached it.

"Hello, Eve Rochorskova speaking. Can I help you?"

"Yes Mr. Mc Intosh, I have been notified about that meeting and I am planning to be there."

"Yes certainly Mr. Mc Intosh. It spells E V E and R O C H O R S K O V A."

"No it isn't H C R O it is C H O R."

"Yes all right. My christian name is Eve. E for evening, V for vicar and E for evening again. Yes Mr. McIntosh it is very easy to pronounce. Almost as simple as any Australian name, did you say? Well, I suppose, you are right. The surname starts with R for raven, Mr. Mc Intosh."

or for the rat I can smell in this conversation already

"The next one is O for ostrich, Mr. Mc Intosh."

I wouldn't mind burying my head in sand to avoid this never ending ritual of name spelling. Why do I bother? Why don't I shorten it? To something simple and easy, something like RAY, yes R A Y.

"The following letters are C for cat and H for house. Yes, I know it is rather long, but it is quite a normal name back home and after all, it is my name. Yes, I do realize I could shorten it by deed poll. As I said, the C is followed by H, just like in Christ, Mr. Mc Intosh."

For Christ's sake, I can just see you. Sitting on the other end of the phone in your three-piece suit, your degree from the local university on the wall, looking important and feeling self righteous about your heritage and about your name.

"The next one is O again, for opinion, Mr. Mc Intosh."

yes, you are full of these. Everybody seems to be. Everybody seems to know what is best for me, how I should feel and what I should do.

"Next comes R for risks, Mr. Mc Intosh."

the risks you take by employing me, no doubt. The years I have spent studying and the degrees I obtained from a university at least four centuries older than yours, are of course inferior and so I am a risk you take.

" No Mr. Mc Intosh, we are not at the end yet, but we are half way through."
"No I am not married, why do you ask?"
"Oh, I see. If I did get married to an Australian, I would acquire a new name and that would make it easier. Is that what you are suggesting, Mr. Mc Intosh?"

well, I do not intend to get married and certainly not in order to make it easier for people to remember my name. No one makes it easier for me, no one ever did. No one ever apologised for their names when I couldn't pronounce them. But then, of course, I was the one who arrived here late.

"The next letter is S for surgery, Mr. Mc Intosh."

I have a vision of a hospital trolley, slowly being wheeled out of the operating room. The lights of the operating theatre are going out, the doctors are washing their hands, nurses emptying and cleaning the bloodied instruments. You are on that trolley, you have undergone a delicate operation. Your head was carefully opened at the cranium, your brain quartered and removed, all but the section retaining your memories. Three quarters of your brain matter was replaced by that of another man. When you wake up, you will be someone else. Someone else, but still with the memories of your own past. You become another person. Your name is now Jacubowitz.

"Yes Mr. Jacubowitz, the next letter is K for ketchup. Oh, I beg your pardon Mr. Mc Intosh, somehow I just got the names confused. No, I can assure you Mr. Mc Intosh, I am with you, yes of course I will continue. The next letter is O for ostrich again, Mr. Mc Intosh."

94

now it will be you, who will hide in the sand, unable to face the daily reality of double identity. The one of your past and the other of your present.

"Then comes V for victory, Mr. Mc Intosh."

I do enjoy it, no matter how imaginary and fleeting it might be.

"The last letter is A for Australia, of course, Mr. Mc Intosh. Yes, Mr. Mc Intosh, believe me I am also glad that it is all over. I will most certainly remember that meeting next Wednesday. Good Bye, Mr. Mc Intosh!"

The First Time

S. Kucharova

"Are we going to be there soon, mum?" the girl asked.

"Yes, very soon" came the reply. The girl was sitting strapped in her seat, watching the houses go by.

It was a beautiful sunny morning and she knew that it was an important day for her. She was going to the pre-school for the first time. Until now she had been minded by their neighbour in the upstairs flat, but recently her mum and dad decided that she should start at the pre-school.

Livia was tingling all over with excitement. She had seen the little school before, when her mum brought her there to fill in some papers. There were toys and children everywhere. Livia remembered that while mum was in the office, she saw the children sitting down on the mat in front of the piano and singing with the teacher. Livia loved singing, she sang to her mother all the time, she knew all the songs her nana taught her. But she didn't know any of the songs the children were singing, she couldn't understand the words, but she liked the tune. She stood there watching them. They were singing in the same words that everyone seems to talk around her when she goes shopping with her mum or when she watches the TV. Ever since they arrived on the big plane, she just couldn't understand what anyone said to her. Just as well that her mum and dad were around, she could talk to them, she loved to tell them what she saw in their new home.

The car stopped at the traffic lights and she waved to the children crossing the road on the way to school. They looked so grown up.

"Now Livia, I can't stay with you for long. You know, I am going to leave you there, don't you? Do you remember what we talked about yesterday?" Livia nodded her head in agreement. "You will be there by yourself only for two hours, then I will come back and we will go shopping to the big plaza you like so much" she said, changing gears. The car moved on.

"Yes" said Livia, "I remember. There will be lots of children and teachers speaking the words I can't understand, but I will stay there because I have to learn.

96

They will be kind to me and daddy said he will bring me a surprise tonight."

Livia now saw the big park which she remembered from her previous visit. Somewhere in the park was her 'little school'. The car stopped and Livia started to undo her seat belt. Mum got out the other side and took her by the hand.

"Look mummy, what a nice playground, so many things to climb on, can I try them?"

"Not right now Livia, we have to go and talk to the teachers" said mum slowly walking toward the small brick house. Livia carried her new school bag, the one that she wanted so much, yellow with a blue front pocket. It had an apple and banana inside and a jumper in case it turned out chilly. The big door opened and they walked in. The room seemed full of people and full of noise. Livia held the hand more tightly, suddenly afraid of losing her. They walked into a smaller room with a tall lady sitting behind a desk.

"Dobrý den. Já jsem přivedla Liviji" said her mum, but all that Livia could understand was 'Livia'. It was all said in the TV language again.

"A', Livije, no pojď sem a ukaž se mi" the tall lady smiled and extended her hand to Livia. Livia didn't understand what the lady wanted her to do, but she felt her mother pushing her from behind and so she stepped forward.

"No ona se bojí, tak ji nenuťte" said the tall lady and smiled again at Livia.

"Já jsem paní Křečková" she said pointing to herself," paní Křečková."

"Ty jsi Livije" she smiled and pointed her finger at Livia.

"Livia" said Livia slowly, repeating the only word she understood.

"No dobře, vidíš, že my si budeme rozumět" answered the lady, smiling again.

Livia looked up to see what her mum was saying to all of this. But her mum and the tall lady were already talking, well, the tall lady was talking and mum was trying very slowly to say something too, but Livia felt that she was very unsure and so she started to worry about her. The tall lady was moving her hands up and down, picking up pieces of paper and giving them to mum, who didn't seem to know what to do with them.

"Tak pojď, já ti ukážu tvojí skříňku, kam ty jsi dáš tašku po každé když přijdeš" smiled the tall lady and again extended her hand to Livia. This time Livia pretended not to see the hand and clung even more to her mother's.

"It is all right, we are just going to see your locker" said her mum and slowly followed the tall lady. As they walked outside the small room, groups of children were standing around small tables involved in various activities. The tall lady stopped at one of the tables.

"Tohle je Livije a její matka. Livije zde zůstane pár hodin" "They are talking about me" noticed Livia, but at the same time her attention was caught by the jars of red, yellow and blue paint, that the children were spreading on the table with their hands. Suddenly, another lady came down on her knees and pointed her finger dangerously close to Livia's face. "Livia" she said and then, pointing her finger towards herself she said: "Já jsem paní Mlochořová" and again smiled.

"Why is everyone smiling all the time" wondered Livia, knowing she should repeat her name, but deciding she would rather not. "Já doufám že se ti zde bude líbit" continued the lady, then got up and walked back to the painting children.

The small locker that Livia was shown stood in the row of similar ones, but each of them had a different picture on it. Livia's had a picture of a cat on it and she knew she would remember it, because after Teddy bears, cats were Livia's most favourite animals. She put her bag inside, making sure that the blue pocket was properly closed and wondered what was she supposed to do next. Her mother finished talking to the tall lady, crouched down next to Livia and got hold of her hands.

"Well, little one, I have to go now. Look at all of these toys here, you can play with all of them. Isn't it nice? Won't you enjoy it? I wish I could stay here and play. By the time you have played with all of them I will be back. Then we will go shopping."

Livia listened, looking carefully into her mother's face. It just didn't sound right. She could feel all the uncertainty inside her no matter how hard she tried to hide it behind her smiles.

"I don't want to stay here" she said quietly, knowing she was breaking the promise she made before.

"But Livia, you have promised to stay here, we did talk about it, your dad is going to be disappointed" said her mum, looking pleadingly at Livia.

"I don't care, I don't want to stay. I want to go away with you" repeated Livia trying to hold on to her even more tightly.

"Come on Livia, you are a big girl now. It will be only for a couple of hours and then I will be back."

"No I don't want to stay here by myself."

The tall lady suddenly crouched down next to mum and put her arms around Livia.

"To bude vše v pořádku, nic se neboj" she repeated in a soothing voice, but Livia couldn't understand what she was saying.

"You have to stay" her mother said, kissed her on the cheek and stood up to go. "I will be back soon."

Suddenly she was walking away from Livia, through the glass door. Livia tried to run after her, but the lady's hands stopped her and she could not move. She tried to get free, but the arms were too strong to let her go and her mother disappeared altogether.

"She is not coming back." A total panic flooded through Livia. "Mum, mum" she shouted and fought with the hands that were stopping her.

"Neboj se, ona zase přijde nazpět, ona jen odešla na malou chvíli. Tak se neboj a přestaň"

But Livia couldn't understand, it was all just a blurr. Her tears came out, she felt like she was choking.

"Mum come back, please come back. I don't want to be here, I will die here, please take me with you."

She scratched the hand that was holding her and when that let go, she ran to the door, behind which her mother disappeared a while ago. "Let me out, let me out." She kicked the door and tried to reach the handle which was too high. "Let me out, please." The door stood solid and closed. Exhausted she collapsed by the door looking into the playground sobbing.

"Maybe she will not come back, maybe she will disappear like her nana and grandad, whom she had not seen since the day they left their old house in the other place, where she could understand what people were saying. Her favourite nana who always told stories better than anyone else.

"Let me out, let me out" she jumped up and kicked the door again and again.

"Livije, přestaň. Když ty rozbiješ ty dveře, maminka je bude muset platit a ona se pak bude zlobit" came the voice of the tall lady. But once again, the words were just a sound and had no meaning. The hands that stopped her from joining her mother were coming close again. Livia felt fear and while watching the hands, she backed away from the door and from the hands.

"No neboj se maličká. Já ti neublížím, pojd̃ sem." The hands, like monster claws, kept coming nearer.

"No go away, I hate you. I want my mum" she tried to shout, but no sound came out and even if the words did come out, no one but Livia would understand.

"No dobře, jak si myslíš" came the reply and the tall lady moved away.

Livia found herself in the corner, her back against the cool wall, crying loudly. She felt she had been abandoned to these monsters. She had been left behind with nothing to hold on to. Then she remembered. She got up and rushed to the other side of the room where the lockers stood.

"Now where was it?" There, the picture of the cat and her bag. Her bag which her mum selected in the shop and put her name inside. It was still there. She grabbed it and pulled it out of the locker. Still crying, she sat on the floor and while holding the bag, she looked around the room. Everyone seemed absorbed in their activities, although Livia caught the tall lady watching her. She pretended not to notice her and concentrated back on to her new bag. It looked so bright and so familiar. The red clips on the blue pocket reminded her of the eyes that her dad would sometimes draw on cartoons to make her laugh. And suddenly, one of these eyes winked at her, just like he would do.

"He will bring me a surprise tonight, he promised" she said to herself, clutching her bag. "I wonder what it will be."

White Sex

Vilma Sirianni

Tick-time in the bush. Tweezers working near my breasts. Only six, and I feel that it is wrong that I must be seen. I loathe these little creatures that find their way to such places. The tick is out and I am left shamed and I hate my father for having seen me. Shapeless and sexless my body is already my embarrassment.

And one day a friend's mother comes to ask the Italian lady in person if I can go to her child's party. My father says no. There will be boys there. Even at eight, boys are a menace. But the hint is that the menace is more in me. Wanting to go means I am bad. So I ache with the wanting.

At school four boys ask me to be their girlfriend. I love it. My friend rides all the way from the beach with her little brother to see me. I feel the displeasure of my parents like a knife and wish they would go.

And puberty comes one Autumn morning. Red and sweet-smelling. No explanations. Only white cloths and warning. Don't let any boys know or see. Not even your father. No modess; just cotton squares hung out on the line. White flags to my womanhood. I try tampons secretly. Mamma is shocked and swears I will never be able to be married and worries.

I learn that my virginity is me. Without it I am nothing. It is all I have to offer as a woman. No man would settle for less. High-school is all-girl, so I have no contact with boys at all. My hormones work on me spitefully and I am aroused to fantasy. I spend hours in front of a mirror. In sexy lace scarves, Mamma's black, church ones I pose, vogue-like. And I think I am beautiful but no-one tells me, so I am never really sure.

The proposals of marriage start to come, keep coming from stranger-men who want my purity without ever imagining the other depths of me. No dates, just marriage offered carelessly. My one love letter is opened and laughed at so my stomach is full to the neck with anger and humiliation.

No is the word. No college or Uni., no parties, no lipstick or shorts, no beach or mini-skirts. No red dresses. Everything is painted with a sexual brush. And my father rips my Beatle poster off the wall and tells me I am immoral.

My sexuality is a bomb within me. I nurture it with my own dreams. A young man knocks on our door one day. A salesman. He tells me I am nice. He asks me out. I say no. Italian girl. You know. He leaves. But he plays in my dreams for a long time.

At twenty three, white-veiled I walk my virginity down the aisle to offer it to a man I hardly know and who I found out later couldn't have cared less one way or the other.

The Questioning of Persephone MacDougall

Zeny Giles

"You will have to help me Kyrea Capsalis," said Persephone to the old woman. "I have never been to the hot baths before."

"Did you never take the waters in Greece?"

"Never. You see, we were poor. We lived with our relatives."

"I have been visiting the waters here now for nine - or is it ten years?" said the old woman. "At the beginning I would come with my own friends. But they are dead now - all dead."

"My husband died six years ago. He was only fifty-three."

"Bad enough to lose a husband - but worse to lose your friends. I could never speak with my husband. But friends - they are something different."

Persephone's eyes had filled with tears. She did not answer.

"We should put on our bathing costumes here and I wear my dressing gown." The old woman pointed to the suitcase. "That long one. It looks like a bedspread. *She* chose it."

"But it is chenille, Kyrea," said Persephone as she lifted the gown onto the bed. "It is all cotton and it washes very well."

"It still looks like a bedspread. But then my body is old - see these flaps on my arms and my legs too. I was a fine figure of a woman once. Now look at me."

Persephone wanted to comfort, wanted to say to the old woman - no, no, it is not so bad - but she was intrigued herself by the loose feel of the skin as she helped Kyrea pull on her black costume over the floppy thighs and buttocks, the thin breasts, the arms with the two shirred pouches sagging from the muscle. It was as if the body's covering was an almost finished layer that should be blown away or burnt like old leaves.

When Persephone went herself to change in the bathroom, she was comforted to feel the spring within her own flesh, to find her body full and round with even a shine on the skin of her shoulders. The darkness which had been the source of humiliation as a girl, had served her well. Her skin, even at the top of the arms where most women begin to show their age, was remarkably firm. She looked at herself in the mirror so long that the old woman was calling. "What are you doing in there? We should go now before the sun gets too hot."

As they walked, Kyrea Capsalis leaned on Persephone's arm. Her steps were slow, even slower than they seemed the night before. "Take these," the old woman said groping to remove her sun glasses. "*She* bought them to cut out the glare but I cannot see if I wear them. Bad enough to need help to walk without being blind as well."

When they had paid and walked inside, Persephone was disappointed to see two hot pools, the water pale blue and clear, like any chlorinated baths. "The sign says we should shower before going in," she said to Kyrea.

"Never mind what it says. Find me a seat. I must rest or I will never have the strength to try the waters."

While Kyrea was resting, Persephone found a cabin, locked away their valuables, showered and came back again.

"The pool in the sun, not the other one," said Kyrea. "It is early and I need the warmth."

Persephone walked with Kyrea to the pool's edge. As the old woman stepped down into the water, she clung harder to Persephone's arm. But even as she stood supporting Kyrea, Persephone was overwhelmed by a new sensation. The sun shone out of a clear sky, the heat encircled her, soaking now inside her, warming her blood as if her whole body was drenched with sunlight.

"Take me to my chair again," panted Kyrea who was shaky as Persephone guided her up the steps and over to the deck chair. She covered the old woman with a towel and craved to return again to the warmth of the water.

They bathed three times, each one a little longer than the one before, but none of them long enough to satisfy Persephone. She felt herself drawn to the heat, to the translucent water which soothed and warmed and even though she began to feel the weariness that came with the heat, she wanted more.

"We must go back now to rest," said Kyrea. "Can't you see how weak I am?"

They made their slow way back to the motel. "I am thirsty," said the old woman. Persephone made tea and they ate the remaining bread and chicken. The old woman lay on the bed. Her intermittent snoring stirred the quiet.

Persephone cleared the little kitchen, hung out the bathing costumes and towels on the outside line and came back to rest on her bed. This warmth inside her was something she had not thought to find.

Sun beating hard on skin. How she would soak up that sun - bathe herself in it - take off her clothes, let the sun warm her breasts, ber buttocks. Open wide her legs and let sun soak into those parts. And all the time the nagging. "We must keep you out of the sun Persephone. Your skin will grow even darker and how will we find you a husband?"

The afternoon ritual began again at three when the strength of the inland sun began to fade a little. They began their slow walk to the baths, rested, dipped into the pool, then out again, while Kyrea found the energy to venture again. Persephone remained tantalised by the water's heat, unable as she was to stay longer.

Back in their room, Kyrea Capsalis, wearied by the bathing,was almost gentle. They sat round the small table and ate boiled eggs and toast with fetta cheese and olives. When Kyrea could not manage to guide her spoon to her mouth, Persephone scooped out the egg into a bowl and the old woman leaned over, feeding herself with shaky hands.

Afterwards Persephone brought a warm flannel and wiped the egg from the old woman's mouth. They sat then in contented silence, the old woman soothed almost to sleep, Persephone watching from the window the red-gold glow turn to darkness. Till rousing herself, the old woman said, "It isn't past seven? I don't want to miss 'Sale of the Century'."

"Ah, do you watch it too," said Persephone smiling. "It's one of my favourites."

"What else do you think I do at my daughter-in-law's place but watch television all day and all night."

By nine o'clock Kyrea Capsalis began to nod again and Persephone prepared her for bed, making sure to remind her about her bladder.

"Don't you start now," the old woman complained. "It's enough that she treats me like a child to be questioned and potted. *Have you done chicha, Mumma?* " she mimicked. And she continued a slow rumbling complaint against her daughter-in-law until Persephone had her changed and in bed and went herself to the bathroom to prepare for sleep.

The day had passed better than Persephone had expected and she felt a growing warmth towards the old woman in spite of her bad temper. Now she felt tired - a different kind of tiredness as if her whole body had worked hard. She would not take a sleeping tablet tonight. She would let her body give in to this pleasurable weariness. She switched off the light and walked carefully to her bed.

"Don't be quiet for me," said Kyrea. "I'm not asleep."

"You seemed so tired at the television."

"I nod off there, but I'm not a good sleeper."

"Perhaps if you didn't sleep so much in the day time."

"It makes no difference. I always have bad nights."

"Nights seem to be the time for worrying."

"And what have you got to worry about?"

"I worry about the rents. If they go any higher I will have to think of moving."

"You don't have a house?"

"I'm in a unit. I pay eighty dollars a week. That doesn't leave me much over."

"A waste of money, rents. Even if you live in one room, it's better to buy it. What have you got after giving over all that money? Nothing - nothing at all." The old woman was quiet for a while. "Don't you have any savings - enough to use as a deposit for a house?"

"When my husband died, I had a few thousand dollars - but it was not enough for a deposit. And now, you see, I have lent it to my brother. He is in Athens and he has children. I help him when I can."

"These relatives in Greece think we are made of gold. You should not have given him so much. And why hasn't he asked you, a widow without children, to come and live in his house?"

"I do not want to go. I do not want to live in Athens."

"He has only one sister - didn't he insist that you should join him?"

Persephone did not answer. The letters told of his need, his house, his children. All these years and he had not suggested she come, even for a holiday. But she did not want to think of it - did not want these worries stirred up again. She got out of bed, went to the bathroom, took a sleeping tablet and resolved that if the old woman spoke again, she would pretend that she was sleeping.

Persephone was growing impatient. She resented standing in the water with the old woman leaning against her now that she realised Kyrea might have held onto one of the handles at the edge of the pool. Persephone had been paid and Kyrea expected her to provide her services.

Once that afternoon as Kyrea dozed, she thought she would go quickly to bathe alone, but she remembered that the old woman had slumped forward in a half-faint that very morning, and Persephone had been the one who had stopped her from falling.

At least she was spared Kyrea's conversation. The old woman rested in her chair after bathing and only spoke when she was ready to venture again.

Persephone began to look closely at the people. Most were women and most were middle-aged to old. There were three or four others like Kyrea in their eighties - their old bodies pale and crepy. The one young couple she could see stood out so clearly. His dark skin was taut and shiny-brown. His wife was fairer with fine soft skin. Their little girl bumped into Persephone and turned to smile, revealing her missing first teeth. Her large eyes were dark and fringed with long lashes.

Even Kyrea Capsalis was roused to speak. "Eine Elinopaedhi," she said with conviction. "She is a Greek child and what a beauty she will be with those eyes."

"And that body," thought Persephone, startled by the child's sleek limbs. She watched the girl's bird-like movements as she toed her way around the hot pool and out to the Olympic Pool, and Persephone calculated that this was the age when she herself had come, an orphan to her aunt. Her mother had been ill and Persephone had been used to running as she liked around the island. She could match the boys in all their games and would go with them each day to swim.

"But she is such a dark little girl," they said to her in Athens. So began the battle. "Persephone, come out of the sun," her aunt would call. "Do you want to look like a little Turk?"

Then as now she was drawn to the rays beating down on her skin and the pleasurable feeling of warmth. In defiance of her aunt, she would seek out the sun - shocking her cousins by taking off her clothes and letting sun soak into her.

"We will tell. We will tell Mumma." But all three of her pale Athenian cousins envied her brown all-over body and her delight as she swam and gambolled in the sea.

It was with some satisfaction that Persephone informed Kyrea as they walked back to the motel that evening. "You know the child we saw with the beautiful eyes. I spoke to her mother when I went to get our clothes from the cabin. They live in Dulwich Hill, but they are not Greeks at all. They are from Turkey."

That night, Persephone decided she would use the remaining chicken to make broth. The soup simmered as she cleaned up clothes and hung out bathing costumes and towels. She had often made chicken soup for her husband. He had liked it strong with rice and plenty of pepper.

But she had not realised how difficult the soup would be for Kyrea. Her hand shook so much that the broth spilt onto the table before she had a chance to get it into her mouth.

"Shall I help you?" she asked, thinking of how the old woman had accepted the warm flannel the night before.

"Am I a child that you should feed me? That's what *she* tries to do. And do you know what else? She sits me to eat in the kitchen so I will not dirty her precious carpet."

And seeing the old woman's humiliation as she spilt the next spoonful, Persephone said, "I've made the soup too thin. I'm going to drink mine out of a mug. I often do this as I watch television."

She poured her own soup into a mug and did the same for the old woman. To cover her victory, she began to speak again.

"Do you know the story of the old man who lived with his children and grandchildren in their home? The man's hands used to shake badly and when he tried to eat his food, he would spill it. His daughter and her husband grew irritated with him and decided to have a special bowl made with high sides so he would not mess the table. Still when he ate, the old man would spatter food so that eventually, his son made him a bench in the kitchen, right away from the dining room. The youngest grandchild was only four years old and he was playing one day with clay. His mother and his father sat admiring him because he was their favourite. "What are you doing, my little one?' asked his father. The little boy looked up and said to them, 'I am making a bowl for you Papa and a bowl for Mumma as well. You will be able to use them so that you won't make a mess when you are old like Buppoo and are living with me.'"

The old woman smiled. "I will tell them both that story next time they complain about me."

As Persephone was drifting off to sleep that night, Kyrea said to her, "I am not so blind that I cannot see that you have been a beauty."

"Yes," said Persephone, without embarrassment. "I was very beautiful - but dark. And when my mother died and I came from Samos to live with my aunt and uncle in Athens, they would make me fair. 'Persephone!' they would call to me. 'Come out of the sun. Your skin will become even darker and how will we find you a husband?'"

"I know those pasty faced Athenian women, frightened that their faces will shrivel if they see the sun. So you married a foreigner because your skin was too dark?"

"No," said Persephone. "If there had been a dowry, the Athenians would have forgiven the darkness of my skin."

"Couldn't your brother help?"

"He was five years younger. What could he do for me?"

"And your aunt and uncle?"

"They had three daughters of their own to provide with dowries."

"So they married you off to this foreigner?"

"They did not protest. And I was happy with him too for he was kind. No Athenian man was ever kind to me."

"And he was handsome - this Englishman?"

"He was not handsome. And he was not an Englishman. He was from Scotland."

"Did he have nothing but his kindness to give you?"

"Nothing else," and Persephone turned her head to the wall and began to cry.

Jamie's kindness could not warm her. She was always cold in the dark council house where they lived with his mother. She would lie shivering in the big double bed with the covers piled on top, trying to make herself warm by thinking back to that bright Athenian light, the heat of the summer sun, the familiar comfort of her language. Jamie would take her shopping and buy her woollens but her body under the weight of the clothing stayed cold and her feet inside the wollen stockings and the thick boots were as lifeless as dead fish. The small fire in the kitchen grate sent out a small ring of heat but did nothing to warm the house's stone cavities. In the bathroom with the old fashioned bath, the water was never hot and she learnt in time to boil a kettle and sponge herself. At work where she and the other women sat at their tailoring, the big iron radiators stayed lukewarm against the cold.

At the end of May, she grew excited at the first clear day. She watched with amazement as the men in the park took off their shirts and turned their white skin towards the sun. But even in summer that sun was not strong enough for her. And when Jamie on one almost bright day took her to the seaside, she was saddened by the pallid sun and the icy feel of the North Sea.

And always clothes hampering her body. Even in bed the heavy blankets stifling any joy in their loving. Convincing her that the reason she did not fall pregnant, was that his seed could not grow inside her in a land so cold and grey.

Now as she lay rather stiffly in bed so as not to wake the old woman, she felt her body cold and lifeless again. She remembered the comforting warmth of the water today, the sun on her face, and her body encircled and penetrated by heat. Persephone resolved that tomorrow she would leave the old woman alone in the deck chair, just for five minutes, so that her body might move with freedom in the liquid warmth.

"You should not have left me."

"Kyrea, you were sleeping."

"I just closed my eyes and when I opened them you were gone. You don't know how I feel when I find myself suddenly alone."

"I'm sorry I upset you but I leave you when I go to find the cabin. I leave you when I go to the shop to buy food."

"These are things you have to do. But to leave me so that you could go to bathe alone. You're paid to look after me. I should have told them last night when they rang."

"Kyrea, I was away for ten minutes - a quarter of an hour at the most. And I could see you as you sat near the pool."

"How am I to know you will not do it again - will not leave me to go off somewhere by yourself? Or perhaps it was not by yourself. Perhaps you are meeting somebody here. You could have arranged it all before we left Sydney. My son pays for you to come, for your accommodation and gives you money so you can look after me, and instead, you go and meet somebody."

" Kyrea, I met nobody. I know nobody here. I have spoken only to the little girl we saw yesterday and to her mother."

Nothing could take away Persephone's joy. And if her fifteen minutes in the water had to be paid for by Kyrea's chiding, it was worth it. When she had stood in the pool with the old woman, her body had been soothed. But when she was free to swim, she revelled in the movement of her arms, her legs, enjoyed the water from the spouts tumbling against her back and her shoulders. And Persephone felt an exquisite happiness burst inside her like a sudden flight of birds. No wonder she had stayed away so long. No wonder she had the audacity to stand more than three minutes under the pouring water. And like some young girl with the secret knowledge of her love, she wanted to show kindness to those who did not share her joy.

She took special care that night as she prepared their meal with slices of ham, bought from the Chinese man at the corner shop, new potatoes and beans.

The old woman's mouth watered at the smell of the potatoes in their skins, steaming hot with melting butter. But it did not stop her complaining. "I do not eat pork," she said at the sight of the ham. "My daughter-in-law told you - only chicken and fish. Now take it away." She continued to look displeased even as she ate most of the potatoes on the table. The butter ran down her chin but Persephone did not dare to bring a wet flannel.

In bed, away from the old woman's resentful look, Persephone hugged her happiness to herself. Joy had come before in unpromising wrappings.

Those red roofs, the harsh glare, the heavy February heat and a dark apartment in an ugly block of brick buildings. Only when he took her by train to the sea, did she begin to glimpse the beauty. They had walked along the high path overlooking the sandstone rocks and the dark blue ocean stretching far far to the horizon. 'And when we have a car,' said Jamie, 'we'll come early to swim.'

Every morning, winter and summer, Jamie would bathe and when the water was warm, Persephone herself would swim in the sea - fearing a little the roughness of the waves. And at the weekend they would explore the bays, the National Park, the mountains close by, or go into the city and take a ferry across to Manly. Not until she had lost him did she know how happy those years had been.

"What was wrong with this McDouga' - this Englishman, that he could not provide for you?" called the old woman from her bed.

"I have told you before he was from Scotland. And he did provide for me. He gave me a happy life."

"A happy life is all very well - but it does not pay the bills. How many years were you in Australia before he died?"

"Eleven."

"Eleven years and he could not buy a house. Do you know my Stavros came in '28 and by '35 we had a house - a three bedroomed house in Kensington."

"It was easier for those who came at first."

"Easy was it? We did not come like the English for ten pounds. We paid the full fare - more than the full fare and we had no help when we arrived. We lived in rented slums with bed bugs, and landlords who did nothing for us but call us 'dagoes' and take our money." She paused for a moment. "And my son - he did not sit still. He has taken what his father left him and has worked as well. Seven houses he owns and a block of offices in Randwick. Do you know that this house where we live now has three bathrooms?"

Persephone's friend Maria had given her a full description of the house, but she gave no answer to the old woman.

Kyrea began again. "Was he a gambler, this husband of yours?"

"He did not gamble."

"Was he a drinker then?"

"He was not a heavy drinker."

"Then what in the devil's name did he do with his money? Or was it you who did not manage. You had no children to feed, to dress, to send to school. Did you put something aside every week?"

"I did save and every year we went for a holiday. One year to the mountains, another time to Surfers Paradise."

"Do you know we didn't have a holiday till 1938? All those years our shop was open every day - even Easter and Christmas days."

"I'm glad we went," said Persephone. "We had those times together."

"That's all very well, but you were the one who told me you lie in bed and wonder how you'll pay the rent. If you'd both been sensible, you wouldn't have to worry about any landlord"

"I'll manage - I'm sure I'll manage."

"You've done such stupid things. You have a few thousand and you give them to that brother of yours who doesn't even care that you're by yourself."

"How do you know that? How do you know what my brother thinks?"

"I've heard he's taken thousands of dollars from you since your husband died. You were a fool to give it to him."

"Your son has paid for me to stay with you Kyrea, but I don't have to listen to you calling me names." And Persephone turned to the wall.

Why did the old woman bully her tonight, intruding on her new happiness, taking away the joy inside her and filling her mind with such a mixture of thoughts. Regrets that she had nagged Jamie because they did not own a house. Regrets that she had given in so easily to her brother - handing over what little money Jamie had left her. Reminding her too of those years when she had sewn for people like Maria and had coveted their bedrooms and their bathrooms and their children. When she wondered if perhaps she would have done better to have married a Greek with a business sense. Now she had become a topic of gossip amongst the wealthy Greeks in their houses in Maroubra and South Coogee. She had trusted Maria but she could see that Maria had talked amongst her relatives - had treated her like some poor unfortunate to be pitied and given the job that nobody else wanted because she was short of money.

Well, she would do the job, but she would bring no more love to it. And she would not be frightened by Kyrea's bullying. Tomorrow she would go as she had gone today to bathe alone. If the old woman decided to complain to the Sydney relatives, she could complain. Let them come and take over.

All day the coldness was between them. Persephone continued to take Kyrea's hand - to have her lean against her in the water, but their bodies were closed to one another. When she had taken the old woman back to sit in her deck chair, she went without excuse to bathe by herself. And conscious of her own defiance and Kyrea's eyes upon her, she moved her limbs, she revelled in her flesh, still supple and still agile.

But that sudden soaring flight had gone from her own breast. And after her second swim alone, she made no other effort to go. Instead she looked around her, and remembering Kyrea's accusation, examined the men at the pool to see if such an arrangement might have been worth it. Only one she found - a tall Yugoslav, perhaps a year or two younger than herself, bald headed with a big framed body and no middle-aged fat. The others with the exception of the thirty year old Turk, were pale, weedy old men.

That evening, Persephone bought a barbecued chicken from a take-away food shop and they ate the dried out meat in silence, escaping quickly to the television characters that had no power to wound.

For the first time since they had come to Moree, the night brought no questioning. If Kyrea was sleepless, she did not speak. And Persephone decided that she would be pleased if the old woman did complain about her when her daughter-in-law rang on the following day.

Persephone lay restless in bed. Not one night had she slept without a tablet. Kyrea was snoring now. Persephone got up, went to the bathroom, took a tablet and was about to switch off the light when she saw the old woman, head high on two pillows, her mouth open. Without her glasses and without her teeth, the shape of the naked skull was so clear behind the skin. What if she should die tonight? What if suddenly that breathing should stop? Would Persephone dare to close the mouth? She felt no fear, only this wanting to know what she would do for finished flesh.

Jamie had died in hospital, the small heart attack leading to another massive one that took him so quickly, she had no part in his dying. Now she wished she had closed his eyes, his mouth, had washed his body, made her last offering to his flesh. She looked again at the old woman. Her head had shifted now and the skin seemed fuller, less paper-thin across the bones. Persephone switched off the light and went to bed.

The wailing tore into Persephone's sleep. The old woman was crying loud, like a child. Persephone ran to her. "Kyrea, Kyrea, what's the matter?"

'When she rings, you must not tell her. If you tell her she will send me away to a home."

"But Kyrea, I would only tell your daughter-in-law that we are finding it hard to get on with one another. I cannot stay with you if you upset me all the time."

The old woman's agitation would not let her listen. "You see, I have to be there in the house to look after him. You do not know her - nobody knows her as I do. She would eat him up. Nearly fifty she is and she wants him in her bed. She would sap him - take away his strength." She pressed Persephone's hand tight. "He needs me to be there. Do not tell her - you must not tell her."

And smelling now the steamy urine, Persephone pulled back the bedclothes and led the old woman to the bathroom. "Sh - sh Kyrea," she said as she began to remove the wet nightdress. "See, you are shaking. We will get you warm again. And do not worry. I will not tell your daughter-in-law."

When she had bathed Kyrea and dressed her in a clean nightdress, Persephone gave her a sleeping tablet and took her back to her own bed, bringing over the extra pillows. Once Kyrea was settled, she went to sort the bedclothes, hanging the wet sheets and the damp blankets over the side of the bath and the shower recess, and sponging the stained mattress.

It was four o'clock. The temperature had dropped and Persephone was shivering. She began to make a bed on the floor but there were no extra blankets. Kyrea was sleeping now with steady, noisy breathing. There was nothing to do but to climb in next to her.

Persephone lay, awkward at first as her body touched Kyrea's body in the narrow bed, but found to her surprise that she was comforted by the old woman's warmth.

Making Connections

Chitra Fernando

As he stood in the kitchen, waiting for the water to boil so he could brew himself a pot of tea, it occurred to Ananda Bandara that though his first name meant "bliss", he had for some time been anything but blissful. The conscious recognition of his despondency only deepened his gloom. The memory of a hearth, fire licking the sides of a clay pot, smoke, turned this kitchen with its gleaming electric cooker, microwave oven and fridge, its clean partly tiled walls into a cold clinical place where machines chopped, squeezed, mixed and cooked within minutes. He looked distastefully at the white walls, bare except for an unframed picture stuck there by his younger daughter, Minoli. The caption read, *The Tree of Life*, Minoli Bandara. He studied it with mounting irritation. As a teacher trainee, of all his subjects, he had enjoyed art the most and had even been considered something of a painter as apparently Minoli now was at school. But was that object in the picture before him a tree? What it looked like was a candelabrum, its red-leaved branches ending precisely to give way to detached leaf-like flames surrounding a glowing orange globe which, like the flame leaves, was quite unconnected to the tree. And why that single purple leaf among all those red ones? It was a crazy picture with no wholeness to it. A jumble of unconnected shapes and clashing colours as Australia was to him.

A stinging heat at his elbow brought him abruptly back to the business of tea-making. He looked around for the canister of tea and couldn't find it. When he finally found it, not in its usual place beside the coffee but next to the curry powder, he couldn't find the sugar; there were no teaspoons in the drawer. His irritation increased. At home in Beruwela, he hadn't ever had to bother about making his own tea. Before his marriage to Leela, his mother had made it for him and then Leela had. He no longer expected Leela to make his tea or his breakfast for him. Things were different here. There were so many things she had to do in the morning: making sandwich lunches for the two girls to take to school and getting her own lunch before she left for work herself at the Epping post office. He had his lunch in the city, where he worked as a clerk in the taxation office.

Ananda found the sugar and a teaspoon and took his tea into the loungeroom, still thinking of Beruwela and Lanka. He hated drinking his tea in this confined space, conscious of every tick of the clock, longed for the wide open verandah of his Beruwela home, for those leisurely early mornings: the chants of fishermen pulling in their nets, loud and clear, then momentarily drowned by the roar and thunder of the Colombo express flashing past between coconut trees, comfortable sounds of household activity, the clatter of crockery, Leela bargaining with a fisherman early with his catch, the deceptive hustle and bustle of an essentially slow-spaced life. It was on such a morning, just like any other morning, that Leela had casually said that nowadays lots of people were migrating. Everything was so much better overseas, food, clothes, employment, education, especially education. Even girls had to be educated these days, hadn't they? And wasn't it their duty to give their daughters the best they could? He'd agreed in principle. But migrating? That was a different matter. Yet he had sensed in himself a faint inner stirring, a disquieting awareness of the monotony of school and household routine, of the smallness of small towns, of mental puddles, a tadpole life. As a trainee-teacher he'd dreamed his dreams, inspired by Ghandhi, had seen himself dedicating his life to the education of the peasants: eating and dressing like them, sharing their miserable huts, sweating in the fields, the founder of a new movement sweeping through Lanka, India, Asia. But nothing of that kind had happened. He had married Leela, had had two daughters, become a householder and a teacher in a Beruwela secondary school.

He looked up from his tea, realizing that Minoli had come into the room. She was rummaging among the pile of magazines on the coffee-table. Ananda was conscious of intrusion, almost discomfort. He watched the girl balanced on her heels in her short uniform, observed her hair sprayed into a fierce cockatoo peak, her blood red nails, a bright predatory parrot. Discomfort grew into distaste.

"Do they allow you in school like that?" He heard the sharp note in his voice.

She shrugged. "There's no regulation against it." Her casualness irked him. She could hardly have failed to realize he was displeased but how indifferent! If he had heard that kind of note in his father's voice at the age of fourteen, he'd have quailed.

"I don't like it," he said and instantly felt foolish. Silence. Minoli rocked gently on her heels. He felt he should say something but didn't know what. It wasn't simply a matter of parental authority, he felt a sudden urgent need to make contact, to communicate. But all he could say again, more loudly was, "I don't like it." Minoli looked up and smiled. She had beautifully even teeth, he noted detachedly, like Leela's. "I don't like your hair," he said a third time. His voice sounded shrill, high-pitched. Minoli looked embarrassed, then concerned. She left the room hurriedly. Ananda stared after her, got up, went to the door. No, he had made enough of a fool of himself for one day. And nothing had happened, nothing really. The girl had done nothing really wrong. He didn't care a hoot anyway about her hair, she could shave it all off if she wanted to. But he couldn't talk himself out of the humiliating feeling that he'd made a fool of himself before his daughter. A minute or two later he heard the door slam and a duet of voices calling out, "We're leaving," and felt immense relief. Almost immediately afterwards he heard another slam and an "I'm off," from Leela, who was leaving early to help a sick friend. He glanced at the clock on the mantelpiece. A quarter past seven. The house was empty, silent. He sat, himself empty, immobile. The silence vibrated, the shrill singing of countless sub-sonic crickets. A thought arose in his mind. "What am I doing here? Why did I come?" He had come, of course, for the children's sake but not entirely. In some undefined way he had also hoped for something for himself, a renewal through new pleasures, an extension of mental reaches. At one time he'd thought of reading for a second degree but totting up other people's millions or their pennies drained him of all his essential energies. He felt cheated, but who had cheated him? There was no-one he could point an accusing finger at. He glanced at the clock again: half past seven. The thought of the office made his stomach turn. Should he send in a sickie? He rejected the idea instantly, he wasn't going to give in to such weakness. He had to go.

Later, in the train buried behind a newspaper like all the others, silent, self-contained in thoughts or print, a familiar pungent smell filled his nostrils, made his mouth water. He looked up. A man, brown and dark-haired like himself, sitting across the aisle had taken out a box of savories. Ananda watched as he offered them first to the man beside him, who wrinkled his nose, shook his head, and then to the two women opposite. They looked embarrassed and mumbled, "No, thank you." The man got out at Strathfield and the women changed their seats. The Oriental looked despondent. He took a few dispirited bites of his food, perhaps it was his breakfast, shut his box and stared glumly at the rows of liver-coloured brick houses flashing past.

Ananda sympathized silently. He too had thought it discourteous, even strange, to eat without first offering the people he was with whatever food he might have had. He remembered with a slight embarrassment the Indian korma and kebabs he'd offer to his office mates, their awkward refusals, half-brusque, half-contrite. Now he ate sandwiches like all the others, even found the salmon and mayonnaise, the curried egg-mixture tolerably palatable. He looked at the man still huddled in his corner, almost went across, then changed his mind. He didn't really want to offer this man his friendship; yet should he make it, his gesture could signal such an offer just as the casual gestures of neighbours and office-associates had been mistakenly interpreted by him. For the first time since his arrival in Sydney, Ananda became conscious of a change within himself. In Lanka he wouldn't have thought twice about offering both food and friendship to a likeable stranger. So many associations, some of the most important, had begun in accidental meetings cemented through the offering and acceptance of food. That's how his friendship with Ariya had begun. A man, obviously a regular commuter like himself, had sat opposite two days running on the daily journey Ananda made to his school in Colombo, his very first appointment. On the second day there had been an exchange of smiles and newspapers. At the Panadura stop, Ananda had hailed a passing *vadei* seller. Remembering that morning's bowl of bland cereal, he thought of those four *vadei* with sharp longing: the brown lentil crusts, each topped with a prawn, nestling close to a fat red chilli. On that morning so distant in time and place, another train, other people, the man opposite had given his four *vadei* in their paper cone a quick glance. And Ananda had said, "Here have one of

114

these." That's how their friendship had begun. Ariya boarded the train first in Alutgama. At the Beruwela stop he'd poke his head out of the window and call out, "Heh, Ana, here, man, here." Two other friends joined them at Kalutara. The journey to Colombo was whiled away eating *vadei*, drinking tea and chaffing each other. Ananda was their special target because of a young woman with a jasmin in her hair, who always sat in the compartment next to theirs. He always looked confused and shy when he caught her eye, which happened every day. Ariya winked and with the others burst into sentimental songs, popular radio hits, which Ananda joined in after a moment's self-conscious hesitation.

The train stopped. Ananda looked up - Redfern already! In a few minutes he'd be at Wynyard. The short walk up Martin Place Plaza, Elizabeth Street, the office and he, a prisoner chained to his desk, barred in by stacks of files and ringing phones. He suddenly felt very tired. The inertia and strange drowsiness weighing him down was increased by the dim compartment lights, the darkness of the underground. Before him rows of bowed heads and beyond close-packed torsos swaying rhythmically at the entrance outside the compartment. He looked at a hand resting on the arm of the seat before him, tufts of brown hair at the knuckles, prominent blue veins. It seemed detached from the body, like the detached leaves of Minoli's Tree of Life.

Light, rows of feet shod in leather, suede, cork-heeled wedgies, stilettos, sandals. Ananda stumbled out, climbed a flight of steps, then another. He wanted to stop a minute, to stand still but was swept forward with other automaton legs, hands with attached brief-cases, a solid purposeful moving mass. No escape. The steady staccato beat of countless feet drove slivers of sound into his brain. He felt battered, bruised though no-one touched him, dazed, mechanically hurrying, hurrying, hurrying. Another flight of steps, a ramp, a street. He looked around him. No red post-boxes, no multistoried office-block. Instead a square clock-tower loomed opposite. Panic, recognition, relief. He'd got off at Town Hall, not Wynyard. Was he to catch a bus? No, he'd walk. He refused to be hurried even if it meant being late for work.

So many big shops, so many elaborate window displays: a group of women in summery dresses. A hand poised in mid-air with a strand of pearls hanging from the slender wrist; the joyous tilt of a golden-haired head, crowned with a little hat of fine Italian straw; a buoyant foot in crocodile-skin shoes....Here was an interior, a dining-room: silver candle-stands mirrored in the walnut table, the chairs upholstered in ivory-white and rose brocade. A change of scene. A beach umbrella: bronzed arms and legs, broad chests, narrow waists with just a brilliant flash of turquoise, ochre, emerald or scarlet signalling bikini or trunks. What had these multistoried temples of fashion and commerce with their elegantly groomed gods and goddesses in their glass-cases to do with him? Wasn't he the same Ananda Bandara whose life's ambition had once been to enlighten the Lankan peasant, to free him from the burdens he had sweated and grunted beneath for centuries? He longed for the bazaars in Beruwela, Alutgama, Bentota, Kalutara - no matter where it was, it was the same: the beggars huddled in their rags, flies, foxy-faced dogs poking into piles of refuse on the pot-holed roads, acrid odours, jostling crowds. He had something to do in such a country, a great task. I must go back, he thought, before it's too late, I have work to do. And he saw himself converting Ariya and his other train friends to the cause, their dedication setting Lanka alight. He would be a second Gandhi. This country, he told himself, as he looked at the window displays, offered every material comfort but a man couldn't live by bread alone. He remembered his experience in the train, that sense of disconnectedness. What it told him was that he didn't belong here, there was nothing significant he could do. Yet he felt capable of doing something significant - but not here.

He walked faster as he turned into Martin Place. A shabby coat and pair of trousers was rooting around in a garbage bin beside the half-moon of maroon seats. Going with coat and trousers was an old man's red beery face covered with stubble, the lips working busily but soundlessly. Perhaps he lived in Martin Place, slept on the maroon seats, living on scraps like the bazaar beggars, a derelict with no family, no home. For one terrible second he saw himself in that old man - the girls married and indifferent, Leela dead. The old man was an omen, a sign-post pointing to instant return. Hadn't the Buddha, then Siddhartha, been similarly directed to his true destiny by one such omen of derelict old age? He had to get on with his life's work without delay, he thought with a mounting sense of urgency as he hurried past the flower-sellers, vaguely aware of splashes of colour, past the glinting waters of the fountain, into his office in Elizabeth Street.

At his desk with a pile of files before him, he was conscious of a longing to talk, to talk of his moment of reawakening, his realization of what he now saw as his proper, his only true goal. He looked at Brian Burrows, whose desk was next to his. Brian was flipping through a file but not too absorbedly. Ananda tried to think of the right question to begin a conversation and then lead gradually up to his momentous realization. It suddenly occurred to him how little he knew of Brian. He talked sometimes of one Sally. Was that Sally his wife? Or his girl friend? These days you could never be sure. Perhaps it was better to be silent. He had never talked of personal matters to Brian before. But now his great realization clamoured for articulation. Anyway wasn't it necessary to give an office-mate some hint that he would shortly be leaving. "Brian, have you always lived in Sydney?" he asked.

Brian looked up. "Oh, yeah, yeah," he said scratching his ear delicately and continuing to flip pages.

"Sydney is your home-town then? Your family have always lived here?"

"Yeah. Came out with the First Fleet."

There was a pause. This was thin ice. Were Brian's ancestors convicts then? Ananda felt mildly embarrassed. His ancestors, as far as they could be traced, had been practitioners of Indo-Lankan medicine. His own father had been a doctor and very respected in Beruwela. Then he reminded himself that people here didn't attach the same importance to ancestry as his people did at home; it would be reasonably safe to continue. "Were your ancestors English, Irish or Scottish?" he asked.

Brian turned slightly towards Ananda. "Heh, what's this? You trying to draw my family tree?" he spoke good-humouredly but Ananda felt snubbed, crushed. He'd said the wrong thing and offended Brian.

"I - I - I'm interested in - in Australian history - the history of the country because I'm now living here," he mumbled. He felt his face burning. Brian nodded. "Got

116

some good stuff in the Mitchell Library - try the Mitchell." He spoke without irony, yet Ananda continued to feel snubbed, deflated as if Brian had access to all the thoughts he'd had as he hurried up Martin Place only half an hour before. In a matter of an instant his falcon-like purposefulness, the swift unerring flight and swoop to a target vanished - he was powerless, small, nothing. He looked covertly at Brian. He was writing, stopped, tore off the page and screwing it up flung it into the rubbish bin. It was something Brian often did but now it brought back a memory, painful then, still painful, with renewed force: it concerned his efforts to save paper. In Beruwela the bazaar urchins painstakingly collected bus-tickets and torn scraps of newspaper to sell to the paper-mill. So at the end of his first month in Sydney he'd taken his old newspapers to his grocer to be used as wrappings. He'd expected Jack to be delighted: smiles, grateful thanks. What he got was a slightly embarrassed grin and then a half-facetious: "Garbos on strike?" He'd stood there hugging a great pile of newspapers, acutely conscious of smiles and stares, feeling such a fool! That's how he felt now, only worse for he now saw how his proposals for peasant upliftment would have been received by Ariya.

"There's a beaut collection of stuff at the National Library in Canberra too. You might like to drop in any time you're there." It was Brian speaking, his mind still on Ananda's interest in Australian history.

"What? Er-er thanks, thank you very much, Brian," mumbled Ananda. Brian's suggestion, casual as it was, warmed him. He felt a small glow of warmth for Brian, he was a good fellow, really. On one occasion Brian had taken him to a bargain sale so he could buy the family a new colour TV to replace their second-hand black-and-white. His sense of deflation and embarrassment slowly subsided, but not the feeling of disconnectedness, of purposelessness.

That noon he didn't lunch with the others. He never said much anyway, just listened, nodded, smiled, though half the time he didn't catch the point of the jokes the others sniggered or guffawed over. Today he wasn't equal to play-acting. It was his flexi-day, so he could have gone home directly had he wanted to but the thought of an empty house frightened him. He decided instead to walk down to the Opera House and sit there for awhile looking at the spread of the harbour.

For a while he leant over the rails looking at a ship anchored opposite, at the gliding dipping gulls settling on the water's gently heaving surface, grey blobs, bobbing up and down as it bellied and subsided, then turned away to sit on one of the benches beside the water, groping in his pocket for his handkerchief. Noticing a group of gulls coming eagerly towards him, he watched puzzled, intrigued. They stood before him in a rough semi-circle, looking expectant. Ananda understood - they were used to being fed and were now wanting food from him. Ruefully, he showed them his empty hands, smiled affectionately, though he knew that was not what they were asking for.

"They're almost human, aren't they? More human than most people, I sometimes think."

Ananda turned round to find that he had been joined by a little grey-haired lady with a round face scored deep with wrinkles. After a moment's silence Ananda said, "Ye-es." Another pause. They looked at the water. Then he heard himself ask, "Why do you say that?"

She hesitated, looked uncertain, then said, "It's my son - what happened to him last week. Two young fellows beat him up - and he wasn't doing anything, just sitting in Denistone Park, listening to the mynahs. You know the mynahs, don't you, what a din they make?" Ananda nodded. "And just then a flock of galahs alighted on the grass in front of him and he was delighted, so glad, you know, that they were so unafraid and then these two fellows set on him."

"Was he hurt?"

"Just a few bruises. He fought back, you see. He's a very kind, gentle man but no coward. It's just that it was two against one, he could've been killed and he's all I've got, you see."

The old lady's story momentarily possessed Ananda. He understood completely that unknown man's self-relinquishment to the moment: the twilight, the chatter of the mynahs, the galahs on the grass, and felt a certain affinity with him. 'What does he feel about it now? Is he angry?" he asked.

"Well, it's strange, though I can see his point, but he says that in some way his experience of violence had made him appreciate ordinary pleasures even more. He feels things more intensely, notices details he's never noticed before like seeing that some gum leaves, those blue-grey ones, are sickle shaped."

"I feel I know your son," said Ananda. He spoke with unexpected warmth.

The old lady looked interested. "Why do you say that?"

"Because I too know how something can make you see things differently."

"What do you mean?"

Ananda told the old lady about that morning: his sense of disconnectedness, his thoughts as he passed the window displays in George Street, the seedy old man in Martin Place and his moment of realization. And as he spoke he saw very clearly that he had no great task to perform and even felt a little ashamed of his fantasy. He just hadn't the makings of a second Gandhi and never had. But he didn't mind the old lady seeing all this. *She* was different from Brian Burrows. Ananda stopped. The gulls feathers wind-ruffled were still there like meditative old men, chins sunk on breasts, neckless, listening. He looked at them as they stood there, attentive, courteous, patient and smiled, feeling relieved of a weight, a burden.

"Yes," said the old lady, "they're better listeners than most people, aren't they? Everybody's so busy, always rushing around, it's hurry, hurry, hurry. Thank you for listening to me and thank you for telling me about yourself." She got up. "Thank you." He watched her till she was out of sight, thinking of their brief exchange. He knew now that he wouldn't return to Lanka, there was nothing of special significance for him to do there. If he did, then he'd very likely think longingly of his brick house in Epping with the tall gums at the back, Martin Place with its trees and its fountain, the elegant city shops....The grass on the other side is always greener was what his mother had said when he had told her they were going to Australia. She had accepted his decision without reproach or resentment. Her image flashed into his mind: a small round-shouldered woman, her grey hair tied back in a little knot, quietly getting about her household tasks. He had had a letter from her only yesterday. She had written to say that the greatest delicacy at the fifteeenth annual almsgiving in memory of his father had been mushrooms, which the five monks who'd been invited had enjoyed very much. The chief monk, who'd returned from Nepal only the week before, had said that the mushrooms that had been eaten there in Buddha's time were still eaten, the kind that grew on fallen bamboos. It had given her great pleasure to be eating the kind of mushrooms Buddha had most likely eaten, she was sure he must have, yet some day these too would die out, for as the monks always said, wasn't everything destined to pass away? What simple things, thought Ananda, gave his mother pleasure. By some process of cunning mental alchemy she charged the trivial and ordinary with point and significance. Wasn't the cultivation of a similar resourcefulness his real task rather than striving to be a second Gandhi? He remembered the man in the train that morning, his fear of involvement with him and then the feeling of affinity through an old lady with her son, whom he had never met and would never meet. He felt himself responding to subtleties, the nuances of experience as never before. No, he wasn't one of the great ones destined to make or unmake history; all he could do was enjoy the pebble on the beach, the leaf on the tree.

That evening was the same as most other Sydney evenings: Leela got through her cooking as quickly as possible to join Preethi and Minoli at their evening ritual of gaping at the flickering shadows on the electronic box. In Beruwela, they used to sit on the verandah talking animatedly of one thing and another; now they were in Sydney, a different time, a different place. Yet Ananda, waiting for the water to boil for coffee, was conscious of new directions, a new purpose. With anything, he thought, you had to create connections, then you understood, coped. "The Tree of Life" caught his eye again. Of course, that was a tree - he was genuinely surprised he hadn't seen it that way before. Those free floating leaves were simply pure pulsating energy given form; the single purple one, a rare flower. The tree gave out light, energy, power concentrated in the glowing orange globe miraculously suspended above it. Ananda felt something like excitement as he looked at the picture. The ancient sages had spent long years meditating in lonely places, struggling to create form out of the formless. He was no sage but he too would make the construction of new meanings, of new forms his chief preoccupation. He thought of the old lady's son, that unknown man he'd never seen who'd made a connection between two unrelated moments and created a new meaning for himself. That was what his mother was doing too. He felt exhilarated as he saw that this was the beginning of his double life: his external life of eating, sleeping, going to the office, mowing the lawn, vacuuming the carpet, putting out the garbage, the life of the householder; and his secret inner life of making new connections, creating new meanings and forms. He thought again of the old lady. Pleasure filled him as he remembered the directness of their brief exchange; it was special, rare like the purple leaf on Minoli's tree. He knew there'd be others like it.

The click of the kettle signalled that the water was boiling. As he made his coffee he heard shrieks of laughter from the lounge, where Leela and the two girls were watching 'Fawlty Towers' on TV. He had no part in their warmth, their laughter. For a moment, he felt a great loneliness and just the faintest twinge of resentment. No, he wouldn't give way to such feelings, he had other things to preoccupy him, the need to make connections which would lead to a renewed engagement with his daughters, with Leela and a new one with the place he now lived in. How and where to begin was the problem. He looked at Minoli's painting again. He would paint, that's what he'd do. Tomorrow, he thought, he'd ask Brian Burrows, the bargains man, where he could get himself an easel, canvas and paints cheaply. He'd first paint the gums in the back garden and then maybe parts of the harbour and the gulls.

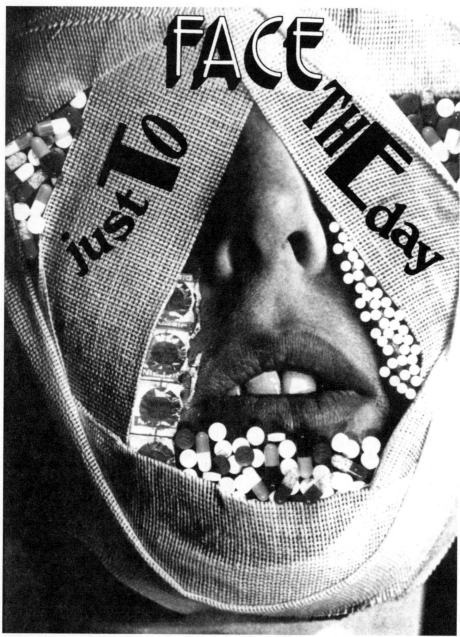

Photo: Peter Lyssiotis.

Finding West Indian Identity in London

Sam Selvon

When I left Trinidad in 1950 I had been working as a journalist with the Trinidad Guardian for five years. During that time I started to write poems and short stories. The first payment I ever received for my writing was a cheque for two guineas from the BBC's Caribbean Voices programme produced by Henry Swanzy, which I treasured for months as a marvel before cashing it.

I was earning enough with the newspaper job to find myself being lulled into complacency and acceptance of the carefree and apathetic life around me. And that was the main reason why I decided to go to London, very much a young man, to seek my fortune.

I wrote to Henry Swanzy, who encouraged the move, and asked him to hold on to a payment of ten guineas the BBC owed me for a short story. I was hopeful that my little writing experience would help, but I was prepared to do anything to earn a living, and stilled my qualms with the tought that I could always return if I did not get one in London.

There was also a feeling for the English countryside and landscape which had possessed me from schoolday reading of the English poets. In the hot tropical atmosphere I dreamed of green fields and rolling downs, of purling streams and daffodils and tulips, thatched cottages and quiet pubs nestling in the valleys. And I wanted to see for myself the leafless trees covered with snow as depicted on Christmas postcards.

In my first English summer I went out to various villages and hamlets and felt the deep and exhilarating satisfaction I had hoped for walking in the fields and woods, which I had dared to dream about while reciting English verse under a mango tree in the schoolyard. It was one of the first things I wrote about. What I miss most about England after living there for almost thirty years is the peace and beauty and inspiration I found in the countryside: the land did not deceive me, as the people did.

Sam Selvon.

My first lodging was the Balmoral Hotel in Kensington run by the British Council as a hostel for overseas students, but it also harboured a number of immigrants from the Caribbean, Africa, India, and other Commonwealth countries. It was my first experience of living among other West Indian islanders, happening in the heart of London thousands of miles from our home territory, and I learned as much about them as I learned about the English, whose ignorance of black people shocked me. This was the country whose geography and history and literature I had been educated upon long before I knew that Port of Spain was the capital of Trinidad, so why did they ask questions like if the people lived in trees, are there many lions and tigers and elephants, and of course, their amazement that I spoke English: How well you speak *our* language! Where did you learn? Once I edited a series of articles by a West Indian immigrant for a national newspaper, in which he said that his white workmates followed him around in the factory, even to the lavatory, to see if he had a tail! Years after it was commonplace to see West Indians working as bus drivers and conductors, the Editor of the *Sunday Times* had to travel to work by bus for the first time, and professed amazement when his ticket was punched by a black man!

The stories - the actualities - are manifest, but I'll only say this: not Buckingham Palace, not the West End or the Tower of London, or the glitter of Piccadilly Circus - not even white men performing menial labor as porters or roadsweepers, nor the fact that there were so many whites who could not read or write - struck me as forcibly, or rather impressionably, as this appalling ignorance about my part of the world, when I had been led to believe that I was coming to the fountainhead of knowledge. Though I was from a small island that might be flicked off the map like a speck of dirt from a jacket, I felt ten feet tall.

My first novel was written while I was working as a clerk with the Indian Embassy. (Even here there was flack - how could I be an Indian if I did not come from India...but eventually I got the job). What I didn't write in the office I wrote in the damp basement room in Bayswater that I was living in at the time. I typed the manuscript myself, on a small portable typewriter a friend had given me before I left Trinidad. I used the most expensive paper I could buy, a kind of thick parchment quite unsuitable for this purpose, but I thought it would impress some publisher. I showed the manuscript to Maurice Richardson, an English writer and critic who had befriended me. Three weeks later he phoned that he had found a publisher. My head spun. A naive Caribbean writer, I had just sat down and written about an aspect of Trinidad life as I remembered it, with no revisions, with no hesitation, without any knowledge of what a novel was, and bam! My first attempt was successful. When the publishers had me to lunch at a French restaurant in Knightsbridge I looked at the menu and forgot all the French I had been taught in Naparima College in Trinidad, except the word 'gateau', so I said I'd have that. But my native wit made me quickly agree when they thought I meant for dessert, and I airily allowed them to order the main course.

I lived in two worlds. Hanging about with Moses and the boys, and at the same time hustling to earn something with my writing, making contact with people in the newspaper and literary world. But more than anything else, my life in London taught me about people from the Caribbean, and it was here that I found my identity. I had no desire to shed my background and cultivate English ways and manners. I was discovering a pride, a national pride, in being what I am, that I never felt at home. That was one of the things that immigration meant to me.

In 1953 I was hospitalised with pulmonary tuberculosis. When I came out the following year I decided to be a full-time writer, on the strength of a Guggenheim fellowship, which took me to America. It was while I was here that the idea of *The Lonely Londoners* came to me. When I got back to London I sat in a friend's house in Ladbroke Grove and wrote the novel there in six months. Two of those were spent wrestling with standard English to give expression to the West Indian experience: I made little headway until I experimented with the language as it is used by Caribbean people. I found a chord, it was like music, and I sat like a passenger in a bus and let the language do the writing.

The critical acclaim when the book was published is there for those who want to see it. Suffice to say that the language and the people added another foot to my ten feet, in spite of a few (inevitable) letters earnestly beseeching me to return to Africa....

It was always a struggle to survive in London, not only because of my non-whiteness, but money. Though I established myself there as a professional writer, I could never write fast enough to keep up with basic expenses like rent and food. The idea of full-time writing was a joke: I was cleaning bars or kitchens in the small hotels around Bayswater: when *Turn Again Tiger* appeared in 1958 I was swabbing out the shithouse at a little private club owned by an affluent Irishman in Paddington who said, "I saw your picture in the *Observer* yesterday, I didn't know you were a writer."

By the mid-70's most of the writers of the postwar efflorescence of Caribbean Literature had left London - England. I myself was growing restlesas. I had spent a great slice of my life inculcating English and European literature and culture, such as eating fish and chips and reading the *News of the World* every Sunday. As a growing boy in Trinidad, from the time of silent movies I was an avid fan because my brothers worked in a cinema and I could get in free. Whatever curiosity or cultural inclination I might have been developing was also due to American films. During recess at school we played cowboys and Indians, imitated American actors: I relate my youthful years with the American music of the 30's and 40's. (There are obvious reasons that the Caribbean has always come under American influences.) It was a part of my memory that needed experience to widen my concepts, and I was not ready to return to Trinidad, or any of the islands - it had to be somewhere on the Continental mainland.

It turned out to be Canada because that was where my wife wanted to go. She had visited relatives (who had immigrated there) a few times and glowed as she compared the standards of living.

We moved, lock stock and barrel. My native wit had thrown out a few feelers for my career as a writer; my name was not entirely unknown in Canada. But to tell the truth, it was almost like the time when I first left Trinidad, except that this was *real* immigration; selling the house, uprooting the family, turning my back on almost 30 years of life in London.

I have never thought of myself as an 'exile' - that word returned to vogue as people shuffled around the world getting settled after the war. I carried my little island with me, and far from assimilating another culture or manner I delved deeper into an understanding of my roots and myself. Immigrating did that for me, and provided the nourishment I could not find in the island to foster my creativity.

I feel I do more for myself and my country by being abroad than I would have had the opportunity to do if I had stayed. I am, in a sense, still visiting abroad. But 'home is where you start from'. And should end from.

The following extracts are from Sam Selvon's novel *The Lonely Londoners* .

The Lonely Londoners

Samuel Selvon

Galahad make for the tube station when he left Moses, and he stand up there on Queensway watching everybody going about their business, and a feeling of loneliness and fright come on him all of a sudden. He forget all the brave words he was talking to Moses, and he realise that here he is, in London, and he ain't have money or work or place to sleep or any friend or anything, and he standing up here by the tube station watching people, and everybody look so busy he frighten to ask questions from any of them. You think any of them bothering with what going on in his mind? Or in anybody else mind but their own? He see a test come and take a newspaper and put down the money on a box - nobody there to watch the fellar and yet he put the money down. What sort of thing is that? Galahad wonder, they not afraid somebody thief the money?

He bounce up against a woman coming out the station but she pass him like a full trolley before he could say sorry. Everybody doing something or going somewhere, is only he who walking stupid.

On top of that, is one of those winter mornings when a kind of fog hovering around. The sun shining, but Galahad never see the sun look like how it looking now. No heat from it, it just there in the sky like a force-ripe orange. When he look up, the colour of the sky so desolate it make him more frighten. It have a kind of melancholy aspect about the morning that making him shiver. He have a feeling is about seven o'clock in the evening: when he look at a clock on top a building he see is only half-past ten in the morning.

When Galahad put on trousers the seam could cut you, and the jacket fitting square on the shoulders. One thing with Galahad since he hit London, no foolishness about clothes: even Moses surprise at the change. Now if you bounce up Galahad one morning by the tube station when he coming from work, you won't believe is the same fellar you did see coasting in the park the evening before. He have on a old cap that was brown one time, but black now with grease and fingerprint, and a jacket that can't see worse days, and a corduroy trousers that would shame them ragandbone man. The shoes have big hole, like they laughing, and so Galahad fly out the tube station, his eyes red and bleary, and his body tired and bent up like a piece of wire, and he only stop to get a *Daily Express* by the station. For Galahad, like Moses, pick up a night work, because it have more money in it. He wasn't doing electrician, but with overtime he grossing about ten so why worry? So while other people going to work, Galahad coming from work. He does cross the road and go by the bakery and buy a hot bread to take home and eat. This time so, as he walking, he only studying sleep, and if a friend bawl out "Aye, Galahad!" he pass him straight because his mind groggy and tired.

But when you dressing, you dressing. Galahad tailor is a fellar in the Charing Cross Road that Moses put him on to and the tailor surprise that Galahad know all the smartest and latest cut. He couldn't palm off no slack work on the old Galahad at all. And one thing, Galahad not stinting on money for clothes, because he get enough tone when he land up in tropical and watchekong. Don't matter if the test tell him twenty guineas or thirtyfive pounds, Galahad know what he want, and he tell the fellar is all right, you go ahead, cut that jacket so and so, and don't forget I want a twenty-three bottom on the trousers.

And the crowning touch is a long silver chain hanging from the fob, and coming back into the side pocket.

So, cool as a lord, the old Galahad walking out to the road, with plastic raincoat hanging on the arm, and the eyes not missing one sharp craft that pass, bowing his bead in a polite "Good evening" and not giving a blast if they answer or not. This is London, this is life oh lord, to walk like a king with money in your pocket, not a worry in the world.

Is one of those summer evenings, when it look like night would never come, a magnificent evening, a powerful evening, rent finish paying, rations in the cupboard, twenty pounds in the bank , and a nice piece of skin waiting under the big clock in Piccadilly Tube Station. The sky blue, sun shining, the girls ain't have on no coats to hide the legs.

"Mummy, look at that black man!" A little child, holding on to the mother hand, look up at Sir Galahad.

"You mustn't say that, dear!" The mother chide the child.

But Galahad skin like rubber at this stage, he bend down and pat the child cheek, and the child cower and shrink and begin to cry.

"What a sweet child!" Galahad say, putting on the old English accent, "What's your name?"

But the child mother uneasy as they stand up there on the pavement with so many white people around: if they was alone she might have talked a little, and ask Galahad what part of the world he come from, but instead she pull the child along and she look at Galahad and give a sickly sort of smile, and the old Galahad, knowing how it is, smile back and walk on.

If that episode did happen around the first time when he land up in London, oh Lord! he would have run to the boys, telling them he have big ballad. But at this stage Galahad like duck back when rain fall - everything running off. Though it used to have times when he lay down there on the bed in the basement room in the

Water, and all the experiences like that come to him, and he say "Lord, what it is we people do in this world that we have to suffer so? What it is we want that the white people and them find it so hard to give? A little work, a little food, a little place to sleep. We not asking for the sun, or the moon. We only want to get by, we don't even want to get on." And Galahad would take his hand from under the blanket, as he lay there studying how the night before he was in the lavatory and two white fellars come in and say how these black bastards have the lavatory dirty, and they didn't know that he was there, and when he come out they say hello mate have a cigarette. And Galahad watch the colour of his hand, and talk to it, saying, "Colour, is you that causing all this, you know. Why the hell you can't be blue, or red or green, if you can't be white? You know is you that cause a lot of misery in the world. Is not me, you know, is you! I ain't do anything to infuriate the people and them, is you! Look at you, you so black and innocent, and this time so you causing misery all over the world!"

So Galahad talking to the colour Black, as if is a person, telling it that is not *he* who causing botheration in the place, but Black, who is a worthless thing for making trouble all about. "Black, you see what you cause to happen yesterday? I went to look at that room that Ram tell me about in the Gate, and as soon as the landlady see you she say the room let already. She ain't even give me a chance to say good morning. Why the hell you can't change colour?"

Galahad get so interested in this theory about Black that he went to tell Moses. "Is not we that the people don't like," he tell Moses, "is the colour black." But the day he went to Moses with this theory Moses was in a evil mood, because a new friend did just get in a thing with some white fellars by Praed Street, near Paddington Station. The friend was standing up there reading in the window about rooms to let and things to sell, and it had a notice saying Keep the Water White, and right there the friend start to get on ignorant (poor fellar, he was new in London) and want to get in big argument with the white people standing around.

So Moses tell Galahad, "Take it easy, that is a sharp theory, why you don't write about it."

Exile of a Non-Exile

Zia Mohyeddin

"One of the biggest phenomena of our times" says Salman Rushdie, an abundantly stylish writer of the eighties, "is the Bomb and the Immigrant." Well I have always disliked the bomb, and come to think of it, the immigrant too. No, that is not entirely true. I have many times fallen in love with the Italian or the Hungarian immigrant in England, but I would be dishonest if I didn't tell you that I resented the Pakistani migrants to England - but that was a long time ago.

In the early fifties when I came to England there were very few of us from India and Pakistan, and yet I remember thinking to myself why the hell is "he" here, what does "he" want? Isn't "he" uncouth? My God "he" is going to let us down. "He" doesn't know which fork to hold when eating his fish. "He" doesn't know how to say please or remain quiet in a library - "he" doesn't know how to behave. I used to feel guilty about it too. I didn't know then that this was one of the most commonplace guilts shared amongst those who choose to live abroad. You've only got to read Forster to find how his protagonists squirm at the insensitivity of the English in Italy.

Migrants we were all of us, but not exiles. Oh yes there were a few. I remember one in particular, a Mr. Ali from Bengal. He had come to England in the thirties. He was a veteran closer to Calcutta than Kensal Rise where he had lived for twenty years. He was merely waiting for things to get better in his province before he went back.

He was a wit and a raconteur. I remember quite a few of the BBC External Services crowd that I mixed with seeking his company. Mr Ali never gave up his style of living. He had no desire to emulate the "English sense of humour" he said. Indeed he was often very rude to the English in pubs and cafes. We took it to be a sign of great individuality and courage.

At that time none of us could speak our minds to the English and I couldn't even to my English friends. I found I could only offer assent when confronted with questions such as our curries are so bland, don't you think? You wouldn't like to stay in this awful climate, would you? What a pity India was divided, surely a mistake don't you think?

As I said I wasn't an exile. And I didn't know I was eventually to become one - of sorts anyway.

I came here in pursuit of a drama. I wanted to be in the Theatre. At that time in the early fifties the idea of a Pakistani adopting the theatre as a profession was as bizarre as a remote control that could change channels on the screen or a microwaved Tandoori chicken. And so although I sensed that it was a very hard task to set up a professional theatre in Pakistan, offering the best of world drama, yet this was the dream I nurtured.

And I wanted to become good, very good as an Actor and as a Director. Oddly enough it did not occur to me that I might not be able to realize my potential on account of my skin. At that time I was convinced that if I could play Lysander or Sir Peter Teazle in a classroom exercise at the Royal Academy of Dramatic Art, then I could also be giving my Hamlet and my King Magnus in the West End.

Skin is something I became aware of later when I entered the world of agents and casting directors - and that vast ocean of an actor's existence - "resting" or non-work. Then it was driven home to me that the parts available to me would have to conform to my skin. This was not done subtly. No matter who I talked to in the profession, a curious accent was tried on me - to make me realize that that was the speech of my people (later on this came to be known as the Peter Sellers accent). The fact that I did NOT speak like this mattered little. It was this post-drama school period of my life when I vowed to myself that for me there was no language other than English that I wanted to adopt, cultivate and live. I became English with a steadfastness that I have not known since. There were rewards I suppose. I became known. I had my name up in lights. I was the first sub-continental to be seen in the company of the Theatrical Knights - and offers came from Stratford and the Old Vic.

It was only when (I thought) I was steeped in English classics, when I was the envy of other actors, for work kept pouring in - and newspapers kept telling me how well I had made it - that I began to realize that there was something false and foolish about my existence. The culture I had discarded began to nag at me. I began to become more and more conscious of my shortcomings. I was growing up, you see.

It was then, at the very time I was first enjoying heady success that I began to probe my own nagging doubts. This was not the dream I had dreamed. The constant need to prove that as a dark-skinned man I was making it in a white world was a hollow desire. What had happened to my ideal of forming a theatre in my own land? Surely, the real test was to try my capabilities and experience in my own country where things had not progressed much beyond my own efforts to form an Arts Theatre Society in Karachi and a Group Theatre Association in Lahore. I had certainly become somewhat disenchanted. I had removed myself considerably from the roots of my own culture - and my upbringing - and my language.

So when the late Mr. Bhutto lured me to come and work in Pakistan I was mentally prepared. In a state of excitement I gave up a lucrative career, a house in

Chelsea (even though it was in the unfashionable part) and a man-servant who had learnt enough English to say "Mr. Mohyeddin's residence" with a great flourish when answering the telephone. This was in 1971.

The years that followed were years of disenchantment and disillusionment. Disillusionment is not to find out that your artichokes are curled even though you are an expert cook, but to find out that you have lost your taste for artichokes. There is no dramatic moment of discovery. It's something that grows steadily. I shall not regale you with the process of my disillusionment for that is a subject for another forum.

The seeds of my exile were sown in my mind the day I was taken off the plane which was bringing me to England soon after the coup that toppled Mr. Bhutto. I was told I could not leave the country. This was like a bolt from the blue. What on earth for? I had staged an outlandish opera a few months before, but surely it wasn't that offensive. I was literally at my wits end.

Wherever I went I drew a blank. No reasons were given. I wasn't in detention, but it felt like it. After a fortnight of frantic efforts on my part to find out how long this restraint would last, I was told, informally, that the Powers that Be were trying to stage a totally different trial against Mr. Bhutto and that my "assistance" would be required. I decided then that if I had to smuggle myself out of the country in a dinghy in the middle of the night I would do so. One of the films that had made a deep impression on me was John Ford's *The Informer*. I was not going to be one - come what may.

That particular trial never took place and I was able to leave Pakistan, but from now on I was emotionally and intellectually an exile. In show business you are only as good or as bad as your last movie - and when I returned in 1977 I didn't have one - at least not for nearly six years. I was fortunate. I managed to get a part or two. And so I had to pick up the pieces of my professional existence this time knowing full well that my work was going to be done in this country and from this country. There was a difference though. I was no longer prepared to give up the feeling for my own language and literature. Perhaps I could do something about spreading that feeling or manifesting it in my own way.

My recent excursions into recordings and readings of Urdu, both prose and verse, have been a new extension to my output. It's amazing to note that even this kind of fairly innocuous work is not being attempted in Pakistan because leaving Ghalib and Iqbal out, nobody knows for sure which of the literary giants might be regarded as suspect by those that matter.

Like most Third World countries Pakistan has always been affected by parochial and sectarian ailments. Nothing new in that but today Pakistan is in the grip of severe tension and strife. Recently hundreds of men and women, children and old people were massacred in Karachi. It was a futile feud, but one that is going to have long repercussions. It was a feud not of the making of Capulets and Montagues, but Big Business which involved the high and mighty. The boroughs and districts of the biggest city are now being controlled by the Narcotics and Arms Mafias. I was stunned by the events of last December. It was a carnage the like of which had not happened since the holocaust of 1947. Amazing motives were assigned. I was told it was an ethnic problem. "Ethnic", I said in disbelief. "Ethnic is a problem we deal with in America and England".

In the last couple of years whenever I have had the opportunity to visit the Land of the "Pure", people keep pointing out to me how much the country has grown materially. They say the per capita income is more than twice as much as in India. We have better roads, more cars, they say. Look, they say, we have colour television in slums, videos in nearly every street. The comparisons with India at every step I find to be odious. It only shows a lingering national neurosis - and the under-developed personality of the country.

Even educated Pakistanis do not seem to be worried that their liberal values are being undermined every day. Public life has become puritanically pompous. One well known religious organisation - well known for its lack of tolerance - has urged science students to free chemistry from the Godless Western civilisation and infuse it with Islamic ideology. H_2O is equal to four visits to the Holy Land - or what?

Creative activity cannot flourish under authoritarian governments. As though this wasn't enough those who are interested in writing or painting, for example, have to avoid being "UnIslamic". Oddly enough the newspapers and periodicals are not so hampered as they were. They now seem to have freedom to criticise the Government, even the Supreme General, but they cannot and will not say a word against religious organisations.

I am not suggesting that all artistic activity has been stifled. There are Theatre Groups for example, but they are in a state of disarray, unable to decide whether to go for a crude comedy, a popular West End success, or to indulge their own whims by doing a Beckett. Sometimes the more committed groups stage performances which attack religious obscurantism, but these are rare and are only staged privately. Classical dancing is *out* by Edict. Nahid Siddiqui, a dancer who has achieved eminence internationally and is perhaps one of the finest exponents of Kathak dancing in the sub-continent (and fortunately my wife), was described in one influential Lahore newspaper as "one who was luring the daughters of the nation into evil ways".

I have often asked myself, "what are we afraid of?" Why do we feel that our morals will be corrupted if we see a dancer on stage or a performance of *Gallileo* in the vernacular? Are we not secure in our beliefs? Do we think that the slightest exposure to Unbelief will shatter the fabric of our moral code?

In my own exile I sometimes agonise over the dark and deep ailments which have enveloped our social and political relationships. I know that in my lifetime the various Islamic sects - the Deobandis and the Barelvis, the Wahabis and a host of others - are *NOT* going to reconcile their differences. I also know that most people will continue to go their ways peacefully and quietly, but will be roused to a frenzy when they feel their religion is threatened. I also feel as long as I live we are not going to stop threatening each other especially where it hurts most. Personally, I wish fervently for a strife-free society, but I know that co-existence of creeds and beliefs can only come about in a state of democracy, which to me means accommodation and tolerance. I am not stating that in Forsterian terms I'll be able to "connect" in a democracy, but only democracy gives me a chance to try it. Unfortunately dictatorship like democracy is a habit (a habit that has lasted twenty-seven years in Pakistan) - and habits are awfully hard to break. There is a school of thought that believes that creative work can only be done by being and living within a repressive society - but I have my doubts.

I do not deny that Solzhenitsyn is a powerful writer, but if he had been able to stroll round to his publisher rather than have the manuscript smuggled out to Switzerland, would the focus of the world's press have picked him out and put him so clearly in the spotlight?

A dissident in exile - a writer for example - has much more power to influence his country from abroad, for these days they often destroy your manuscript along with your spirit when you are languishing in jail.

There is a danger though: exiles cannot accept (by nature) that their exile will not come to an end. They tend to become romantics because they have to see a rosy dawn at the end of the tunnel. Their view and work can, therefore, become a little removed from the reality of the situation that exists in their country. One has only to look at elements in the Polish community in Wolverhampton resisting the English language and any Anglicisation and waiting innocently to return to a Poland unchanged in fifty years.

It is now a little more than ten years since I became involved in the philosophy, if not exactly the politics, of Exile. It is not a long period, but long enough to ruminate and reflect. There is no doubt in my mind that I have been able to work more and it has been untramelled by such considerations as "will it be acceptable?" -- "is it safely Islamic enough to be admired?"

Maybe I was too old when I accepted my own exile. I could have had more fire, more passion if it had come about earlier.

Listen Mr Oxford don

John Agard

Me not no Oxford don
me a simple immigrant
from Clapham Common
I didn't graduate
I immigrate

But listen Mr Oxford don
I'm a man on de run
and a man on de run
is a dangerous one

I ent have no gun
I ent have no knife
but mugging de Queen's English
is the story of my life

I dont need no axe
to split/´up yu syntax
I dont need no hammer
to mash/´up yu grammer

I warning you Mr. Oxford don
I'm a wanted man
and a wanted man
is a dangerous one

Dem accuse me of assault
on de Oxford dictionary?
imagine a concise peaceful man like me/
dem want me serve time
for inciting rhyme to riot
but I tekking it quiet
down here in Clapham Common

I'm not a violent man Mr Oxford don
I only armed with mih human breath
but human breath
is a dangerous weapon

So mek dem send one big word after me
I ent serving no jail sentence
I slashing suffix in self-defence
I bashing future wit present tense
and if necessary

I making de Queen's English accessory/to my offence

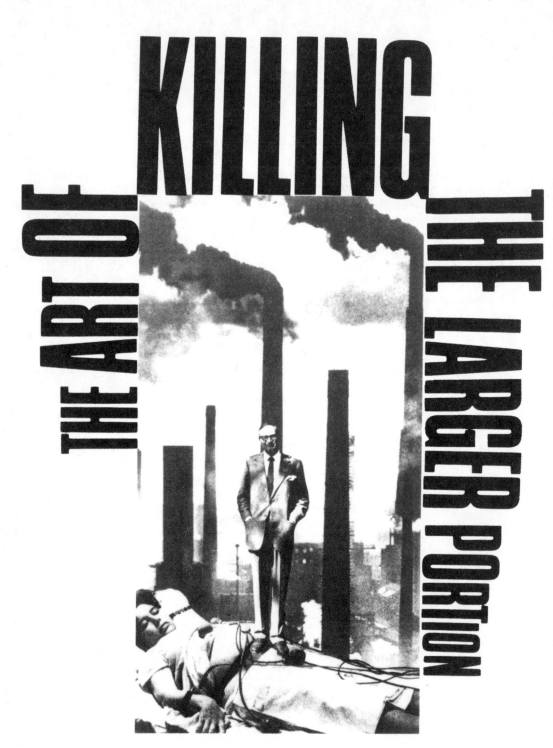

Photo: Peter Lyssiotis.

From Care to Cambridge

David Dabydeen

I was sent to England in 1969 to join my father who several years earlier had divorced my mother in Guyana and emigrated in the hope of finding work in London. He had been a cruel man to her and the childhood memory of his selfishness influenced my relationship with him in England. I disliked and feared him the instant he collected me at Heathrow. He was a short, pot-bellied, dark-skinned East Indian. I had not seen him since early childhood. I was now thirteen. He shook my hand wordlessly at the airport. We headed for a place called Balham, mostly in silence.

He had married again, to a red-skinned Guyanese - a move up for him in the chain of being, given the relationship between status and shades of colour in the Caribbean. She was jealous of me on behalf of the four children she had borne for him. I was a threat to her family, a part of her husband's past she naturally resented. I felt sorry for her, and at the same time puzzled by her weakness in tolerating the excesses of my father.

Looking back after eighteen years I suppose I was too severe in my hostility to him. He had come to England in the 1960's as an ambitious immigrant, had scraped together a few paper qualifications by long study at night school, and had gradually acquired nice possessions like a house and car. His aggressive material and sexual greed was motivated by insecurity. Being a mere boy I did not understand his own trauma. It was only much later that I discovered that he had once spent a few months in Brixton jail on a charge of fraud. I believe he forged some papers to get some money. The experience was deeply shameful to him, he had never allowed anyone to visit him in Brixton jail. And he never spoke of it afterwards.

London was bewildering. There was the marvellous novelty of brick houses joined end to end, snow, eating with a knife and a fork, deep red apples, wearing a school blazer with shirt and tie, and buses to ride on. The white people were frightening to begin with. On the second evening I ventured outdoors to view the street and was overtaken by a middle-aged white man wrapped in a winter overcoat whose skin, in the streetlamp light, took on a ghostly, grey appearance. I have never been so terrified in England since as I was that night by the sight of that pale image of death.

School was exhilarating. The white boys swore in a shocking way, every other phrase being "fuck your mother". They also seemed academically dull for white people. They disliked the Asian boys because we (although Indo-West Indian, I was quickly recategorized as a Paki) were far better at the subjects than they were. I took particular delight in beating them at English. What was enjoyable about the English school was the relative lack of competitiveness and the more liberal environment. In Guyana, education was the only means of escaping from the mud, and city school places were few, so the boys were deeply selfish and competitive, refusing to share ideas or information or books. The teachers there beat us to learn, and parents beat us at home whenever the term school reports came in. Some of us became adept at crammming and cheating so as to survive. England however was wonderfully relaxed, being more luxurious than Guyana, but yet many of the English youth were extremely ignorant. They showed little curiosity about the world outside England, but were quick to invent derogatory names to call foreigners. A small percentage of them possessed a humane spirit which marked them out. These boys appeared to be in advance of any of my schoolmates in Guyana. Although just thirteen or fourteen, they read novels, some wrote poetry or composed songs which they played on musical instruments. They were generous of spirit, ready to share (indeed encourage) ideas and make friends. The oddest group were the black British children who were not only dull but surly with it. I was accustomed in Guyana to highly motivated schoolfellows, Afro and Indo-Guyanese, who worked hard to be top of the class. The brightest boys in my school in Guyana, those whom I looked up to almost in awe, were Afro-Guyanese. In England, however, the British-born blacks were startlingly dull and deemed by the teachers to be aggressive trouble-makers. There was obviously something wrong with England itself, which created the gap between the achievement of the West Indian and the black British child.

A series of resentments and disagreements ended with my stepmother packing my clothes one night and telling me to leave right away. My father, unsure about what to do, counted out thirty one-pound notes and said he was sorry things didn't work out. I was about fifteen, so the Social Services were called in as soon as I reported to school the next morning. I had spent the first night in clichéd fashion on a park-bench in Tooting, stuffed with pound-notes, defiant and at the same time anxious about what to do next.

I spent the next three years in Care, when, in 1974, I went up to Cambridge where I became not so much a *displaced* as a *misplaced* person. It was a most uncomfortable experience. I simply didn't have the money that social life in Cambridge demanded. A basic Cambridge accoutrement such as a dinner jacket or suit was beyond my means. This was 1974: the student revolts of the 1960's had died totally, and the undergraduates had reverted back to rugby matches, wine-tasting parties and the wearing of monocles. Had I gone to Cambridge in the 1960's I would have been at home in its environment of studied underprivilege and working-class solidarity. Nor was there money for the obligatory grand tours to Europe that undergraduates made during the "vacs". At the beginning of each term the undergraduates would be greeting each other with cries of "how were your vacs old boy" (truly), and the tedious pattern of intellectual tourism would follow. Being a West Indian, and barring finances, I had no desire whatever to see Europe. England was our destination, and England was enough. I imagined that Europe would be more or less the same as England - shops, art galleries, motorways and even more white people. It was only in the mid-1980's that I made my first venture into Europe - to Spain, which turned out to be remarkably like back home in its peasantry, "colonial" architecture and tropical climate - and only because the trip was being paid for by the British Council. I was going to a Commonwealth Literature Conference in Spain as the poet representing Britain, travelling first class for the first and last time in my life, and with a most generous hotel and spending allowance. I read some creole poems at the Conference, about the barefooted folk of Guyana, then flew back in style to England.

During the so-called "vacs" I would escape from Cambridge to bedsits in Tooting or Clapham South, and to the safe retreat of the nearest dole office. It was a relief to be surrounded by black people again, and ordinary houses, after the gorgeous human and architectural ambience of Cambridge. The experience of being in Care even took on an almost romantic glow. True, I was always desperately short of money whilst in Care, but had developed a fine strategy of survival based on a mixture of study and theft. The study involved a devouring interest in books of history and literature; the theft was a means of acquiring the books. It was not a widespread or habitual crime, and my secret removal of books from various public libraries would not have bankrupted these institutions. Of course I stole food as well, when supplies were severely low, sometimes from Sainsbury's, but more often from the Asian shop at the top of my road. I preferred to patronize the latter because the shopkeeper was a nice man in a turban and over the months I had struck up a vague friendship with him, talking about cricket or India or illegal immigration or the weather. He practised his English by these long conversations and I was happy to help out. I felt sure that if he had caught me walking out of his shop with tins of sardines or jars of marmite he would not have called the police. Sainsbury's was another matter. I also stole the odd sums of money. I once broke into the coin-meter in my room and in an adjoining room in the bedsits where I lived. These years in Care were a mixture of the sordid and the street-wise, perhaps more the former than the latter, and yet they deepened my sense of human values. Although poor, the people of South London were not always mean and closed. There were many deeds of kindness from various Asian people to whom I will always be grateful. Their deprivation bred a kind of adolescent idealism in me, so that *things* , edible and desirable as they were, didn't ultimately matter. What mattered were ideas which things merely facilitated. I had become so foolishly moral that when I broke into the first coin-meter I actually left in the empty coin-box an I.O.U. scribbled on a piece of paper, with my initials.

I went up to Cambridge at the age of eighteen to read English Literature, but really wanting to become a priest. I spent three unhappy years there, never going to the lectures or seminars. In my three years I went to two lectures altogether, the first to see what they were like, the second to impress a visiting girlfriend by taking her to a lecture on art. The first occasion was painful: a balding, loathsome lecturer in robes spat out eighteenth century philosophy for an hour, his talk full of insulting asides about his colleagues at the University. I felt deeply stupid since I could follow neither the topic nor the gossip; terrified too, engulfed by a horde of white youth who obviously understood the lecture since they were scribbling away vigorously in their notepads.

I retreated to the University library where I spent many exhilarating hours of solitary reading and researching. I dwelt mostly on Hardy, Lawrence, Strindberg and Medieval poetry, reading practically all I could, including the very obscure books (Hardy's play for mummers, for example, more or less forgotten by all). Hardy's peasant people and country fatalism reminded me, sentimentally, of back home, and I liked too the fact that he was scorned socially by eminent gentlemen like Sir John Galsworthy for having muddy boots. Lawrence was a rebellious outsider who made it to the top out of hunger and contempt. He was passionate and imaginative, and his celebration of pre-Columbian consciousness was despised by clever, necktied establishment figures like Eliot and Wyndham Lewis. Strindberg's dramas were shrieking, delirious, yet deeply idealistic, imbued with obsessions about inviolable purity which were strangely Hindu. Finally, Medieval poetry. Reading *Sir Gawain* was a startling moment. The sheer energy and nakedness of the dialect instantly recalled the "pre-civilized" language of Guyanese creole. By total immersion in this "Western" literature, one was able to sense its universal roots, or at least borrowings from our cultures, and read them through Guyanese eyes. When I read Sam Selvon's novels for the first time two years later I could hear Chaucer's chuckle in every passage.

In the summer of my second year at Cambridge I borrowed some money and returned home to Guyana. My step-father was apparently dying of liver problems (he had been an alcoholic for twenty years or so), so I had to go home, as the eldest son, to sort things out. Home in fact was not the whole of Guyana, but a small wooden town therein, audaciously named New Amsterdam. No one outside of New Amsterdam knows or cares about the existence of the place (it has a population of 14,000 or so) but it was a town which bred writers of international reputation like Edgar Mittelholzer and Wilson Harris. Guyana from the air was a vast green spread scored by lines of rivers. From the protected cabin of the aeroplane it looked a pleasant enough landscape. As the plane swerved and lowered towards the tarmac I recalled the sense of dread that most Guyanese feel about the jungle that is our abode. Most of the country is bush. We live on a thin strip of coastland, with the impenetrable bush behind us and the roaring Atlantic before us. On a clear day you can see nowhere. We are an island not only in our own country but in a continent - an island not in terms of geography, but in being the only English-speaking country in South America. Prospero's magic was wondrous. When I was a boy I had read a newspaper story of some New Amsterdam men who had ventured deep into the bush in search of gold. A few months later one stumbled out, half-starved and babbling. The rest had either been bitten by snakes or struck down by diseases and accidents. They had found nothing, but the one man was determined to come out alive to speak the truth. He made the headlines and the story was carried for weeks. The story reminded me of the Tarzan films which so enraptured us in our boyhood, packed into the pit of the Globe cinema, a cinema appropriately named since it offered one of the few chances of viewing the world outside of New Amsterdam. The cinema was located, also appropriately, at the edge of the mouth of the Berbice river which flowed out into the ocean beyond.

It was the same river I had to cross on my first homecoming. The steamer, left over from the days of British rule, careered from one river bank to the next loaded with old Morris Oxford passenger cars and market goods. A crippled man smelling of rum dragged himself along the aisles. He sang Hindi songs and shoved his hand at the passengers. A little girl, barely five, followed him with an alms box in which I placed a few coins in remembrance of our shared Indianness.

David Dabydeen.

Coolie Mother

David Dabydeen

Jasmattie live in bruk -
Down hut big like Bata shoe-box,
Beat clothes, weed yard, chop wood, feed fowl
For this body and that body and every blasted body,
Fetch water, all day fetch water like if the whole -
Whole slow-flowing Canje river God create
Just for *she* one own bucket.

Till she foot-bottom crack and she hand cut-up
And curse swarm from she mouth like red-ants
And she cough blood on the ground but mash it in:
Because Jasmattie heart hard, she mind set hard

To hustle save she one-one slow penny
Because one-one dutty make dam cross the Canje
And she son Harilall *got* to go school in Georgetown,
  Must wear clean starch pants, or they go laugh at he,
Strap leather on he foot, and he *must* read book,
Learn talk proper, take exam, go to England university,
Not turn out like he rum-sucker chamar dadee.

Chamar - low-caste.

Coolie Son

(The Toilet Attendant Writes Home)

Taana boy, how you do?
How Shanti stay? And Sukhoo?
Mosquito still a-bite all-you?
Juncha dead true-true?
Mala bruk-foot set? Food deh foh eat yet?

England nice, snow and dem ting,
A land dey say fit for a king,
Iceapple plenty on de tree and bird a-sing -
Is de beginning of what dey call 'The Spring'.

And I eating enough for all a-we
And reading book bad bad.

But is what make Matam wife fall sick
And Sonnel cow suck dry wid tick?

Soon, I go turn lawya or dacta,
But, just now, passage money run out
So I tek lil wuk -
I is a Deputy Sanitary Inspecta,
Big - big office boy! Tie round me neck!
Brand new uniform, one big bunch keys!
If Ma can see me now how she go please.....

Catching Crabs

Ruby and me stalking savannah
Crab season with cutlass and sack like big folk.
Hiding behind stones or clumps of bush
Crabs locked knee-deep in mud mating
And Ruby seven years old feeling strange at the sex
And me horrified to pick them up
Plunge them into the darkness of bag,
So all day we scout to catch the lonesome ones
Who don't mind cooking because they got no prospect
Of family, and squelching through the mud,
Cutlass clearing bush at our feet,
We come home tired slow, weighed down with plenty
Which Ma throw live into boiling pot piece-piece.
Tonight we'll have one big happy curry feed,
We'll test out who teeth and jaw strongest,
Who will grow up to be the biggest,
Or who will make most terrible cannibal.

We leave behind a mess of bones and shell
And come to England and America
Where Ruby hustles in a New York tenement
And me writing poetry at Cambridge,
Death long catch Ma, the house boarded up
Breeding wasps, woodlice in its dark-sack belly:
I am afraid to walk through weed yard,
Reach the door, prise open, look,
In case the pot still bubbles magical
On the fireside, and I see Ma
Working a ladle, slow-
Limbed, crustacean-old, alone,
In case the woodsmoke and curry steam
Burn my child-eye and make it cry.

144

Interview with Caryl Phillips

Some West Indian writers like Wilson Harris, V.S. Naipaul and Roy Heath have been living in Britain since the 1950's. You represent the younger generation of Mustapha Matura, Linton Kwesi Johnson, David Dabydeen, and David Simon. Is the writing of Harris, Naipaul and others of their generation important to you?
The writers who were important to me initially were Black American writers. I think that's largely because Ralph Ellison's work was available in Penguin Modern Classics, and James Baldwin was an international figure. The fact that Lamming, Selvon and Harris actually existed was more important to me than what they were writing. The only works of their generation with which I had any real empathy were those which related to England, like *The Emigrants*, and *The Lonely Londoners*. Works which were rooted in the Caribbean meant nothing to me. I felt much more in tune with the urban jungle that Ralph Ellison or Richard Wright would describe, because I lived in an urban jungle myself.

One of my first impressions of your work was that it didn't fit in with my experience in the West Indies. But it did fit in with the black Americans, that is to say with the experience of black people who had been westernized in a metropolitan, Euro/American context. It seems to me that your writing deals with black people who have been westernized in a similar context.
Actually a novel which I now recognize as great, but which didn't mean anything to me at first was *In the Castle of My Skin*. Richard Wright's *Black Boy* was phenomenally important to me because I could understand the pain and the kind of despair of actually growing up in the South, and having to deal with white society. Lamming's book about a Caribbean childhood was remote from me. Richard Wright's book was closer, since it was about being young and feeling utterly out of tune with the society around you. What you had in *In the Castle of My Skin* was somebody growing up and feeling more or less in tune with his society. Lamming was describing the process of growing up in the bosom of that society with the rich smells, outdoor nature and so on that was very remote from my experience.

Lamming and Selvon wrote about West Indian immigrants arriving in Britain with false expectations and attitudes. These immigrants encountered

145

discrimination. Their warm, sunny temperament and flexible Caribbean attitudes came into conflict with more rigid, metropolitan, cultural habits. The result of the conflict was very negative. but at least there was hope that things might change later on. Your books give me a sense of what has happened later on, after your characters have lived in Britain for twenty years. They still think about going back home to the West Indies. There is still the same rage, bitterness and dissatisfaction with Britain. Have twenty years made no Difference?

In terms of the British attitude towards black people and towards West Indians in particular, I would say it has changed since Lamming's day when there was curiosity, then hostility. In my day, I think it's almost hostility distilled. There is no longer any curiosity about black or West Indian faces. I think part of the anger or hurt which may permeate my work comes from the fact that when I look at the life of my parents, and people of my parents' generation, I feel they have been given a terrible deal by Britain. I also feel that it would be very difficult for me to see a future for myself in England if I were a married man with children. Looking ahead now, I feel slightly angry and upset at the fact that I won't be comfortable bringing up another generation of West Indians who, because of intractable British attitudes will have to go through the same problems I went through. These are the same problems that were depicted in *The Lonely Londoners*, thirty years ago.

In *Where There is darkness*, Albert is preparing to return home. In *Strange Fruit* Alvin goes home, and in *The Final Passage* , Leila is set to go back to the West Indies.

My novel *A State of Independence* concerns a man who has spent 20 years in England, and also decides to go back to the Caribbean. The novel actually begins with him on a plane circling over an island. It's about the first three days he lands back there, and his reflections on how he's spent 20 years in England. He's not kept in touch with anybody. He feels some bitterness about England, and a kind of romantic love toward the Caribbean. In him I have pulled together all the strands in my plays, and really tried to examine that question of what happens to the man who tries to go back. I have never really felt that it is possible to go back. I think that the bleakness perhaps in some of my work comes from the fact that if you do reconcile yourself to the fact that it is not possible to go back, then you are there, and the situation that you are in is, unfortunately, an unhappy one. That's the experience of my generation in Britain. If you look at the work of any of my contemporaries, it's all to do with a struggle to be accepted, which, in 1986, and given the pioneering work of those writers who came over in the 50's and 60's, and also the work of my parents and other parents like them, makes it all seem futile. The question leaps out; "When will it end?"

No responsible person could suggest emigration from Britain as a solution - "repatriation" as Enoch Powell calls it. But, in an artistic way, you could dramatize a situation which encourages people to consider the implications of "repatriation".

West Indians in Britain who have a memory of the Caribbean - most West Indians, anyway - have the idea at the back of their minds that perhaps one day they can go back. The problem is when you don't have any memory of the Caribbean, and you have been told that's where you are from. That's why Alvin in *Strange Fruit* goes back to the Caribbean, returns to England, and actually discovers that the Caribbean is not for him. So it's a real problem to have no memory of the Caribbean, and it's a problem to have a memory of the Caribbean. If you seek to discover the Caribbean as somebody growing up in North America or Britain, then nine times out of ten you will be disappointed.

I seemed to detect parallels between your work and Paule Marshall's. Did reading Brown Girl Brown Stones *have any effect on you?*
I don't really think it did have an effect on me because, I wasn't aware of Paule Marshall in the context of West Indians in the States. I am now aware of her perhaps because *Brown Girl* has been issued again, but also because of people like Jamaica Kincaid who are beginning, from an American point of view, to look at the West Indian experience.

You seem particularly hard on women in your books, for instance, the mother, and the girl Shelly in Strange Fruit. *I feel a little uncomfortable about the intensity of victimization which the women seem to suffer in general - both black and white. In the case of Shelly, she seems so utterly hopeless. Nobody wants her: her parents don't want her. I agree the boy's mother offers her something and gives her the key to her house. But Shelly's situation is one of real desperation.*
I am glad you mentioned the mother giving her the key. The mother could never convince her two sons of how much she loved them. Somehow, by giving Shelly the key, I wanted to show her capacity for love. The second thing is that I wanted to examine the whole question of a mixed relationship. The third thing I attempted to depict was the situation of being desperate. I wanted to throw into relief the idea that all black people are directionless, and all white people have a sense of purpose and direction; because you know as well as I do that there are white people who are more screwed up than black people. Those three factors contributed towards my presentation of the mother and Shelly.

Don't West Indian women take an excess of blows, both emotional and physical, in their relationships with men?
I don't know enough about West Indian domesticity in the islands. In the case of West Indians in Britain, it seems to me that the women have taken more blows than the men. In the Caribbean it is a matriarchial society. When you come to Europe it is a patriarchial society. I think that that quite vicious shift from one form of behaviour between men and women to a different form in Europe produced, in a lot of West Indian minds, an irresponsibility which no generation could afford to endure. After all, when you are going through problems of adjusting to a society which in many ways and forms is rejecting you, it doesn't really help if your father, for whatever reason, decides to leave the family.

This happens quite often, doesn't it?
Well, it happened in my family. But that's not why I am concerned with

147

examining it. I am concerned because there are very few of my West Indian contemporaries in England, who actually grew up in a stable family background.

Another first impression I had of your work was that you knew the metropolitan situation of the black minority and white majority very well. The relationships, the language, dialogue, and tensions, were exactly right. Then I noticed that in writing about people in the West Indies, there was the same authenticity. Your control of two contrasting milieux really impressed me. I suppose the fact that you have deliberately gone back regularly to visit the Caribbean might help to explain it.

When I sat down to write a novel set totally in the Caribbean, *A State of Independence*, I felt that, as a contemporary Caribbean novel, a sizeable proportion of it must be related to the politics of colonial independence. I think my publishers and perhaps people who read it were very surprised, because they assumed I would go on from *The Final Passage* to pick up the story of what happens ten years later, not necessarily with the same characters, but that I would bring my sensibility further and further into England. In fact, the reverse has happened. I do feel, for a number of reasons, that I desperately want to address the Caribbean situation, as much as I do the British one, and for me it is a matter of research quite frankly. It is a matter of exposing myself to it.

I would think there is a difference between experience that is learnt or researched and experience that is lived, that you grow up in. I wonder that I don't detect a difference in authenticity between your rendering of these two types of experience.

I don't think the two types of experience are considered by my contemporaries in Britain. It is not in David Simon's work, or Linton Kwesi Johnson's, or the work of any of the younger playwrights. Nobody addresses the Caribbean at all. It's difficult to explain to people that I was born in the Caribbean, whereas three of my younger brothers weren't. But I always felt that that got me through nasty times at school and some of the prejudice. I have always clung to the fact that even though I hadn't visited the Caribbean as a mature person, I did have somewhere else. Maybe if I had been born in Britain, and not had to go through my childhood with the knowledge that I was born in the Caribbean I may now be addressing the British situation with more vigour. But for me it has always been a safety valve against the "rivers of blood" type of speeches, against social pressure. It has always been something which has kept me sane, the fact that I was born in the Caribbean. I will always pay my dues towards that.

If you were born in England and wrote the type of literature which largely addresses the problems of minorities and so on, how limiting would you find that? What exactly would be the limitation? Authors who write like that are performing a social function of setting injustice right, or expressing protest against injustice.

I suspect it would be totally limiting. I think it would be impossible or, at the very best, extremely difficult for me to address the situation in Britain only. To limit myself to Britain only for my subject matter would mean that I would be seen as a protest writer, merely as an extension of the university sociology faculty. I don't think it would be possible for me to be seen as a writer "per se". Linton is a very good example of this. He feels very much as though he hasn't even begun writing, despite his established reputation. He doesn't feel he knows his craft. That's perhaps another reason why I'm not prepared to limit myself to the British situation because, eventually, there will come a time when the idea of rage - which is what Baldwin was talking about when he criticized Richard Wright - the idea of rage would become my theme.

That itself would be limiting?
That, in the end, would probably stifle whatever talent I have.

Since you mentioned this question of rage, I want to bring in Naipaul who has also studiously avoided rage as his main theme. This has made him greatly hated or at least controversial. But I don't see in you that emotional hostility towards Naipaul that I detect in many West Indians and West Indian writers?
No, because I think Naipaul's talent is unquestionable. But he made a decision or perhaps he didn't make a decision - perhaps he didn't have a choice of how he wanted to be. But he's been consistent in it. He's never actually strayed into the territory of becoming a spokesperson. He's never jumped on a convenient platform. He has remained detached, and you have to respect the man for his consistency. I don't particularly like Naipaul's view of Africa. I certainly don't like his views on the Caribbean; but I do respect his talent and his consistency. But he doesn't bring out any bile in me, because I don't feel he's interested in the areas I'm interested in. Writers are very territorial animals, and I think I could understand why a Lamming or a Selvon might feel very bitter about a man of their own generation achieving the stature that Naipaul has. Economically, he must be comfortable for the rest of his life. When people hold a festival, for example, and they need someone who has written from the West Indies, they are more likely to pick up the phone to Naipaul than they are to Lamming. After a while, it would piss me off if I was Lamming. But Naipaul is not a competitor in my area.

From the beginning of Where There is Darkness, *there is a flashback, with constant interchanges between contemporary and past action, throughout the play. Where does that technique come from? Are you following a particular trend in contemporary drama?*
The play was inspired structually by *Death of a Salesman*, in which Arthur Miller tried to examine the life of a man who is dangling by a string, and the string is about to break. That's the dramatic situation, and the only way you can textualize the man's life is by seeing what happened before. It is a very convenient dramatic structure, theatrically, from a West Indian point of view, because it looks great when you first see the kind of gloomy, cold English lightening, then the sets and stage revolve, and suddenly it's bright, Caribbean sunshine. Dramatically, the technique is much more powerful when you are given two cultures and two different types of sunlighting. Of course the very term "flashback" comes from the cinema. Arthur Miller's career was deeply involved in the cinema as well.

It's all right to say you were born in St. Kitts, grew up in England and that now you are recovering the Kittician experience so that you can consider both your British residence and St. Kitts origin in your work. But the fact is that you live in Britain; you publish in Britain. People will call you a British writer. You will be compared with the people writing in Britain today. How do you see your position "vis a vis" native British writers?

As I said, writing is very competitive. My development as a writer runs parallel with the development of younger British writers. I look at what they publish and I think I'd better make sure my next book is up to scratch. So I do feel an affinity with contemporary publishing in Britain. However, I think it is an advantage to be liberated from some of the nonsense and parochialism produced not only by living in Britain, but by British incestuous publishing itself. I feel I have a territory or subject matter which is more international than that of my British contemporaries.

Your British/Caribbean perspective gives you an advantage over them?

A huge advantage. But this affinity for black subjects and writing is only one thing that distinguishes me from my British contemporaries. The other thing is a group of novels which affected me when I was growing up. These were novels by David Storey, Alan Sillitoe and John Braine who dealt with the problems of growing up in the working class. Those novels affected me because they portray class and cultural dislocation that I could relate to very easily. When I look at the work of my British contemporaries - people like Ian McEwan and Graham Swift, who are still in their thirties and who are fine writers - their subject matter doesn't engage me in the same way as the subject matter of novelists who came a generation before them. So it's not simply because they are British; it is also their subject matter that distinguishes me from them.

Your position is unique in that you can write with equal conviction from within British as well as Caribbean society. When Naipaul tried to write from a British perspective in Mr. Stone and the Knights Companion, *I don't think he was nearly as successful as in his West Indian novels.*

Yes, but my uniqueness places a special responsibility on me. both Caribbean and British societies have may things wrong with them that need to be examined and exposed. I can see historical connections between the two societies, and I can see contemporary reverberations between them. I also feel very comfortable. culturally, in both societies. I can build bridges, and help to cross-fertilize the two. Given the history of slavery, of colonialism, political and social subjects which I think I am probably in a good position to explore.

Frank Birbalsingh interviewed Caryl Phillips in London in 1986

Caryl Phillips.

NOT DIRECTLY CONNECTED WITH A PRODUCTIVE PROCESS

Photo: Peter Lyssiotis.

152

Policeman Cleared in Jaywalking Case

Claire Harris

The city policeman who arrested a juvenile girl for jaywalking March 11, has been cleared of any wrongdoing by the Alberta law enforcement appeal board.

The police officer contended the girl had not co-operated during the first five minutes after she was stopped, had failed to produce identification with a photo of herself on it, and had failed to give the policeman her date of birth.

The case was taken to the law enforcement appeal board after the girl was arrested, strip-searched and jailed in the adult detention centre.

- *Newspaper report*

(In the black community "to signify" indicates an act of acknowledgement of sharing, of identifying with.

The girl was fifteen. An eyewitness to the street incident described her as "terrified".)

Look you, child, I signify   three hundred years in swarm around me   this thing I must   this uneasy thing   myself the other   stripped down to skin and sex   to stand   to stand and say   to stand and say before you all the child was black and female and therefore mine   listen you walk the edge of this cliff with me at your peril do not hope to step off safely to brush stray words off your face to flick an idea off with thumb and forefinger   to have a coffee and go home comfortably   recognize this edge   and this air carved with her silent invisible cries

Observe now this harsh world   full of white works   or so you see us   and it is white   white washed male and dangerous even to you   full of white fire white heavens white words   and it swings in small circles around you so you see it   and here I stand black and female   bright black on the edge of this white world   and I will not blend in   nor will I fade into the midget shades peopling your dream

Once long ago   the loud tropic air   the morning rushing by in a whirl of
wheels   I am fifteen drifting through hot streets shifting direction by instinct
    tar heel soft under my shoes I see shade on the other side of the road   secure
in my special dream I step off the curb   the sudden cars   crash and jangle of
steel   the bump   the heart stopping fall into silence   then the distant
driver crying "Oh Gawd! somebody's girl child she step off right in front of me,
Gawd!"

Black faces anxious in a fainted world   a policeman bends into my black gaze
    "where it hurting yuh? tell me!" his rough hand under my neck   then seeing
me whole "stand up let me help yuh!" shaking his head   the crowd straining on
the sidewalk   the grin of the small boy carrying my books   then the
policeman suddenly stern "what you name girl?"   the noisy separation of cars
    "eh what you name?" I struck dumb   dumb   "look child you ever see a car
in plaster a paris?"   dumb   "tell me what's your name?   You ever see a car
in a coffin!"   the small boy calling out my name with such shame

Now female I stand in this silence   where somebody's black girl child
jaywalking to school is stripped   spread searched   by a woman who finds that
black names are not tattoed on the anus   pale hands soiling the black flesh
    through the open door the voices of men in corridors   and in spite of this
    yea, in spite of this   black and female to stand here and say   I am   she is
    I say to stand here knowing   this is a poem black in its most secret self

Because I fear   I fear myself and I fear your skeletal skin the spider tracery of
your veins   I fear your heavy fall of hair like sheets of rain and the clear cold
water of your eyes and I fear myself the rage alive in me   consider the things you
make even in the mystery of earth and the things you can an acid rain that shrivels
trees   your clinging fires that shrivel skin   This law that shrivels children
    and I fear your naked fear of all that's different   your dreams of power your
foolish innocence   but I fear myself and the smooth curve of guns   I fear
    Look, your terrible Gods do not dance nor laugh nor punish men   do not eat
or drink but stay a far distance   watch the antic play of creation and cannot
blink or cheer   Even I fear the ease you make of living this stolen land and all its
graceful seductions   but I fear most myself   how easy to drown in your world
and dead believe myself living   who stands "other" and vulnerable to your soul's
disease
Look you child I signify

Placing Truth or Fiction

Aritha van Herk

Holland's insistence in my life was a slow revelation to me. In my childhood, Holland was the "old country" or "home," a collage of myths that tangled themselves together, inseparable and puzzling. Stories of Holland I sorted into the same category as the other stories I knew - fairy stories and stories in books, tales that I assumed were true but distant. Holland stories had a degree of intensity that surpassed the others, a tinge of immediacy that stiffened my delight in story, made me hesitate at their mystery. They were not true, but they were too true. They occupied a period when I had not existed, when my life had been in question. It is inaccurate to say that my parents' stories made me uncomfortable, but they did make me doubtful, apprehensive. I wanted to believe that my muddy and brash world was the only world, all others story. But the confusion between story and reality was inevitable, inexorable. The confusion became reality, another story, another fact.

The first imprints were the massive generalizations around me; my parents, when asked the origin of their heavily accented English, would reply "We're Dutch." It was easy, glib; I parroted it. "I'm Dutch." I was not Dutch at all, I was pure Canadian, gothically Canadian, already picking up the lilt of central Alberta, the grimace of the face when a word is pronounced in the litany of farm parkland, a western inflection to my way of walking, of holding the head. Still, it was tempered enough by the poor English and gradualy bastardized Dutch around me, by the heavy oak furniture and heavier Calvinist doctrine, for me to find myself different: when I stepped inside the Grade One door at Edberg School and looked around at that pack of children, some snivelling and some frozen, some whirling dervishes and some politicians already, I absorbed in exactly thirty seconds exactly how different from them I was. The "old country" had done it. I would never be pure.

That is perhaps why I came to rely on story for a dependable reference: it was infinitely more realistic to thumb a variety of story versions and choose what appeared to be most acceptable than to expect to rely on actual verity. When you are a by-product, a hybrid, an off-spring of transience, you learn the limits of facts and replace them with fabrications. The past, the present, the future, are all magnificent fabrications, pedestrian as they may seem.

The bare facts were clear enough. My parents left Holland in 1949 and arrived at Halifax by boat on April 1, April Fool's Day. They travelled by train from Halifax to Alberta, and stayed there, working as farm laborers until they bought their own farm in 1956. I was born in 1954. Facts.

My parents are now prosperous and retired; they go to Hawaii and Arizona, sometimes even to Holland, where they return from quickly, breathing relief, to pronounce that Holland has gone to the dogs. They are, they say, satisfied. When asked why they immigrated to Canada, they reply that they wanted to give their children better opportunities than they would have had in Holland. If so, their wishes have been granted: all their children are professionals, we all have university degrees. Still, this reason is a lie, I know - a clear and faithful lie. And so do facts merge themselves into fabrication. All has become fiction, an after-the-fact rationalization, as most history is. Well, that is not surprising, it is to be expected in families who have the opportunity to alter their past, to improve their position.

The cultural effect, however, is enormous. Imagine a country as this country is, peopled by characters who have abandoned their setting and who seek to plot their own story in a new way. They choose to displace themselves, to surrender the familiar while they are busy changing the familiar, rearranging it to suit the story. Curiously enough, because they make the choices, they are happy, if not always satisfied with their story, and the effects of displacement only begin to appear in the children or grandchildren. Some people would say that it is only a matter of adapting to a new environment, or adjusting to custom, of learning a language. I maintain that it is much more profound, a displacement so far-reaching that it only vanishes after several generations. At least, it was for me. I learned that the world was fiction and fiction was refuge. The only way to survive was to verify the content of language, of what was said or written, all the time; verify it not for truth, but for fiction. In language, in words, one could find the outlines of a world. I became, out of a love of lies and a desire for truth, a writer of fiction.

It is language, after all, that accomplishes displacement. Emotion and idea have some influence but without language they do not exist - we could not even name them. And it was language that made me aware of the displacement, that spelled it out. I suppose that my first language, what I heard my parents speak, was Dutch. I do not know if that is true because I do not remember and my parents claim not to remember either. English, the English of the prairies, was all around me, and it took over, lay on my tongue like a stone that needed to be spitted out. My parents were conscientious immigrants who learned English quickly (beginning with my oldest brother's grade one reader) and spoke English, gradually relegating the Dutch to a secondary role, diminishing it to a slang-filled and pared-down *taal*. I could not speak it; I could understand it if I tried, but I knew I could not speak it.

Then, when I was twelve, some family came to spend the summer with us. They spoke only Dutch, nothing but Dutch, not a word of English at all. It was a curious summer. I was at first tongue-tied, unable to communicate, but then I discovered that the words formed themselves on my tongue, the language was there. I *knew* the language, it had rested in my head somewhere like a still pod, waiting to blossom, waiting for the opportunity. I had never learned it, but it was there.

It was a gift; it was also a curse. The displacement I thought I had circumvented was there in me all along in the language I carried around, the words I knew, but did not know I knew. That epiphany, that realization, consolidated my pact with fabrication, with fiction, The only verities are words, language.

My Dutch is poor, of course. My grammar is spotty and my intellectual vocabulary is not extensive. Still, it exists within me and that is what matters, what keeps me at the fabulation of words of my own. We are all products of different moments of truth or fiction, and that is mine.

Aritha van Herk.

Interview with Lotfi, Fadhil and Ahmed

Connie Relsted and Anna Rutherford

All three were asked to tell about their life story before coming to Denmark.

Lotfi   I come from Libya. I went to a boarding school where people learn a job. First I went to school for ten years, and then I learnt to be a carpenter, a furniture maker. We were about two hundred pupils who finished at the same time, and after that they found us jobs. I started work with a firm when I was seventeen. We were three people working together and we made furniture and sold it to the market. This was the only job I had before I left Libya.

Ahmed   I also come from Libya, and I went to school for about 15 years, and then I started to work in a tobacco factory as a mechanic, repairing the machinery. I also went to England to do some courses in mechanical engineering, and later I went to North Korea. After some time back in Libya I was called up for the army. It was then that I left my country and went to Denmark.

Fadhil   I come from Iraq, and I only went to school for six years, as my father was very poor, and I had to work. We were six of us, and as my father was very old, my older brother and I worked to keep the family. I started to work in a cafeteria when I was eight and continued there until I was ten. Later I worked as a truckdriver until 1971, then I was in the army for four years until 1975. After that I worked as a seaman for an Iraqi company until 1984, when I came to Denmark.

Why did you come to Denmark?

Lotfi   I went to England for a year to study and learn English, and during that year I met a Swedish girl who became my girlfriend. After my exam I went to visit my girlfriend in Sweden. I took the train and went through

Germany and into Denmark, where I got off at Aarhus and stayed here for a month, because I liked it. It has a different atmosphere from England. Then I continued and went to Aalborg where I stayed for a year, working in restaurants. After that I returned to Aarhus, because I liked it. I made many frieds here, found a place to live, so I stayed. I never got to Sweden.

Ahmed I never thought I would leave my country until I was called up for the army. I decided that I did not want to join the army. That was the only reason I left because I had my job and my family, and I enjoyed all that, but I did not want to join the army, so I thought I would travel. I had a ticket to New York from Tripoli, because I wanted to go to the US to study more, but on the way I visited a friend in Copenhagen for the feast of Ramadan, and I fell in love, so I wanted to stay here.

Fadhil I came to Denmark because I didn't like the system in my own country. We don't have freedom. I had been in the army for four years and they wanted me to stay on longer and longer. The war between Iran and Iraq has gone on for seven years now. The government in Iraq looks at the people as animals, they don't care about them at all. I found out how I could get on a ship sailing from India to Denmark and I did that. We stayed in Copenhagen for about two months, and then I found out it was nice here, so I stayed. To get away from fighting all the time I was prepared to be a refugee.

Have you found any difference between the attitude of the authorities and of the people towards you?
Lotfi When I came here a long time ago I felt welcome. You found a job and then went to the police to get a visa, and you did not have any problem. This was in 1970 and people acted politely and were helpful, if there were language problems for example, but now they have changed, maybe because there are many more foreigners or because many young people do not have a job.

Ahmed When I came here it was only possible for me to stay if I got married, so after I got married I got a visa, and I started going to the school. I came here in 1980, and things were different from when Lotfi came, but I like it. As Fadhil says, the government in my country does not care for the people. I think it is the same in all the Arab countries. This means the father must take care of the family like in my family. My father was always thinking about his family, he thought about his children, about how we were going to get food and clothes and where we could live. He did not think about getting an education or listening to the news about the country. All he thought about was how we were going to manage, because he had a lot of children, twelve. So it was very different when I came here. I can understand why it is as it is in my country. There are many people who know about politics, we are human beings too, but many, like my father

159

for reasons I have just explained, do not care who is the president, and that is why we do not have democracy. They are afraid all the time, because they do not understand politics. They work, earn money and take care of their family. Personally, I don't have any problems with Danes. The worst thing about it is the weather. I now understand why the Danes are less open than our people.

Fadhil   I find that there is a great difference between the Danes and us. Here, people can do anything they want, at home people have to make a choice between one thing or another.

What did you find most different in this society/culture from your own?
Lotfi   Here people are free. They say what they want, you know. Nobody stops them. At home if I say something against the government I go to jail, but here you can say anything. At home we may not say anything, but we still think, within ourselves. People here are isolated. We all have big families, lots of brothers and sisters, and we help each other, but here you do not have that. I have many Danish friends, both from school and from sport, but if you have a problem, and you want to talk to them, they are always a little bit reserved, they push you away a little bit.

Ahmed   Well, the really big difference I see between my country and here is the women. It was a big surprise to me. Here the women are very open, and in my country this is not so. I am thinking about the mother. I don't really feel that the woman is really a mother for her children here in Denmark. In my country even if my mother had a problem with my father I never heard her say to me or my brothers and sisters: 'Oh, shit, this man I live with, your father is really bad', but here it is different. The mother talks to her children. These are things I miss from my country: the family and the women whom I think are better than here. When you sit with a group of Danish women you talk about everything, you know, but when there is just the two of us you see the really big difference. There is always jealousy between the man and the woman in Denmark. It is like a war. It is not love. I don't think that there is real love between men and women here, that is my opinion. so I miss the women at home. Here there are a lot of nice-looking women, but the situation is not like home for me. I am not asking for obedience I just want a situation where people are not constantly fighting each other. But I can see how the Danish men treat the Danish girls and I feel sorry for them. At home marriage is for life, not for a try.

Lotfi   I lived with a Danish girl for six years, and I still live with a Danish girl, but I don't like this war between menandwomen. I love my wife, and she loves me, but we don't carry on this war, we share a home and work, and I accept that. There are some things I don't agree with. In our country when we marry, we marry for life. We don't think 'I will try to live with this woman for two or three or five years, and I'll see what happens'. We don't

160

do it that way. When we marry, we marry, even if we have not seen each other before. There are a lot of people who do not meet before their marriage, so they don't marry for love, but when we get together, something creates love, and we have it together as long as we live, so we do not have the problem which other countries have of separation between husband and wife. Here I see too much of that.

Fadhil I miss relationships. That is something we have, not only in my country, but all over the Arab world. You watch families visiting one another, any time they want to drink coffee or eat, but that does not happen here. Sometimes I get very nervous, because there are people here, who don't like us, who don't like foreigners. I often hear in the street, in a bar, or on the bus: 'Foreign worker, what the hell are you doing here?' That makes me mad, that is why I just borrowed money from the bank and bought a car, I simply don't want to hear it from the people, so I am just going from home to work and back home in my car, that is all...

Have you met racism here?
Fadhil I have met bad people and good people. Some people don't like to help you. Some people push you because they hate you, they don't like foreigners, but not everybody is a racist, no, many people are very nice.

Lotfi It all depends. People here move in groups. If, for example, you try sport you will meet nice people who will like you, but if you walk in the street where nobody knows you, people will hate you because they hate foreigners, and they will say 'go home' or words like that. People should talk to us and then they would understand us. But they don't. They just say 'Oh, foreigners, I don't like them.' Here in Aarhus there is very little racism, not like in Copenhagen or Aalborg and Esbjerg. I think it is because here in Aarhus there are very many foreigners, Turks, Iranians, Iraqis, Pakistanis.

Ahmed I won't say it is racist here, but there is a lot of jealousy. The Danes think they have a good life, and they look to see how we, the foreigners, can manage that. I will give you an example. When I drive my car, people look at me, and I can see that they think that they pay my rent, they pay for a car for me. They look at you, I feel, and at the same time they don't look at you. I am not talking about racism, I am talking about jealousy.

Have you made a lot of Danish friends? Are you invited into Danish homes?
Lotfi Yes, we have friends, not very many, five or six. We see each other sometimes, and sometimes they come here to the restaurant. It is a foreign restaurant, and they like us. Sometimes they invite us home. I have visited many Danes and been with their families, because I was married to a Dane. If you meet someone, and they buy you a beer, and you start talking, then maybe they get to like you, even though they didn't at first, because of what

they read in the newspapers. We are from another culture, and maybe they are interested in learning something about it, and so they invite you home. Many young people go to school or study or travel, maybe to my country, and when they return, they bring with them some small habit, like a food recipe, which they try to imitate. Many people travel for six months or a year, to Turkey, Morocco or India, and there they meet people from the countries they have visited and become friends.

Ahmed I can't say whether I have friends here or not, because the way I know who is a friend is different from here... I make friends with girls, because it is easier to discuss things with them than with Danish men. When I say friend, I mean friend. In my country we have a saying 'Your friend is your back.' When you have a good friend you have a really strong back, but that is not how I see it here.

Have you tried to integrate into Danish society or have you tried to keep your own culture intact?

Lotfi   Fifty, fifty. I was grown up when I came here, but my children who were born here learn more about Danish society than mine, I can never be Danish because of so many things, for example the question of friends which we were discussing before. So it is very hard to be a Dane. I tried, but it is impossible.

Ahmed There are a lot of things I don't like about Danes, so I don't want to try to be like them. Even if I did try, it would be impossible.

Fadhil I agree with Lotfi and Ahmed. There is a difference between real friends and friends you just have a good time with. In my country a friend is more like a real brother, in fact he is more than a brother, because my brother I may only see at home, whereas you are together with your friend all the time. Some years ago people would invite you into their homes, but not now. A lot of people think that their tax goes towards paying for the refugees, and they resent it, but that is not quite true. A lot of the money for refugees comes from the United Nations or Geneva.

Lotfi   People will invite you home, but they are always cautious and a little afraid of the foreign culture. There is also the language problem. If I speak Arabic with a friend Danes can't understand it, and they feel left out.

What do you do to teach your children about your own culture?

Lotfi   My children have grown up here, and they learn Danish ways from their mother, kindergarten, and school. But they know where they come from, and they have many friends among the children of my friends, and when they visit them they see their way of life. So it is fifty fifty. You can't put pressure on them, because they are very young, and if you did they could become disturbed. But you can try. I try very hard to teach them the

162

language, and when they grow up, maybe when they are sixteen or seventeen they will think: I have a family in the other country. Then they will choose.

Ahmed I am happy my daughter has a mother, but I try to make my daughter understand my culture. I always talk to her in Arabic, even if she answers me back in Danish. In that way language should not be a problem in the future if she goes to visit her grandparents in Libya. Then she can see how we live there and how she lives here with her mother. It was very different between parents and children when we grew up in Libya to what it is here. It is a different upbringing. They speak differently to their parents and I try to make my daughter understand.

Are you planning to spend the rest of your life in Denmark?
Ahmed No.
Fadhil No.
Lotfi No.

Lotfi I was not in Libya during the revolution, because I travelled before I came here. After I had been away for ten years I tried to go back. I was divorced and had problems, because, as we said, we did not understand each other, so I was fed up, and I packed my bag and went back to Libya. I still have my Libyan passport, and I have a large family back there. But the regime had changed, and after about nine months I returned to Denmark. If the regime in Libya would change, I would go back.

Fadhil I'll never be a Dane.

Ahmed It is the same with me. Even if I decided to spend the rest of my life here, I would never be like the Danes, I will always be a foreigner.

Fadhil I hope to go back, but it is very difficult for me. I arrived here as a refugee, I had lots of problems with the Iraqi government and with the Danish government, so it is impossible for me to go back to Iraq, but I am not going to stay here in Denmark.

Do you miss your own countries?
Ahmed Yes, of course.
Lotfi Yes, of course.
Fadhil Yes, of course.

What is the worst thing here, and what is the best?
Ahmed I think the best thing is the system here in Denmark, and the worst thing is the people when they get drunk. They become quite different people.

Lotfi The best thing is the freedom, and the worst thing is the difficulty in getting to know anybody and making friends.

Fadhil It is really nice here. But it is the same for me as for Lotfi. I like to talk to the men, but it is very difficult. When the Danish men get drunk they like to talk and talk and talk. But otherwise it is very difficult. I don't know what it is. Perhaps they are scared.

Ahmed This is something that happens to me a lot. When a Danish man is on his own he will talk to me, but if he has his girlfriend or his wife with him he won't even say hello. Perhaps he is scared because he thinks that Arab men always want to take his wife, or what do I know?

Fadhil He is scared.

Lotfi But as you can see for yourself Arab men are as kind and polite as other men, so the Danish picture of us is not valid for everybody. There are good and bad people everywhere.

Select Annotated Bibliography of recent texts which deal with Migration and Racism in Great Britain.

FICTION

Sam Selvon (Trinidad), *The Lonely Londoners*, Longman, London, 1972. The classic work of fiction that deals with the experience of the West Indians who immigrated to England in the 1950s. See also by Selvon, *The Housing Lark, Ways of Sunlight and Moses Ascending*. All of these tragi-comic works are concerned with the simple everyday lives of ordinary Caribbean immigrants in London.

George Lamming (Barbados), *The Emigrants*, Alison & Busby, London, 1980. George Lamming belongs to the same generation as Sam Selvon and his novel *The Emigrants* traces the fate of a group of West Indians who go to England in search of a 'better world' in the 1950s. For one of the best tragi-comic accounts of the West Indian experience in London see Lamming's short story, 'A Wedding in Spring' in *Commonwealth Short Stories* edited by Anna Rutherford and Donald Hannah, Dangaroo Press, 1979.

Caryl Phillips (St. Kitts), *The Final Passage*, Faber, London, 1985. This novel also tells of the great immigration from the Caribbean to England in the 1950s. The novel, which won the £ 2,000 Malcom X prize is beautifully crafted and intensely moving and depressingly lacking the comic relief of Selvon's novels. Phillips belongs to a younger generation than Selvon and it is possible that his bleak view can be related to the fact that the racist situation in England has deteriorated since Selvon's time.

Joan Riley (Jamaica), *The Unbelonging*, Women's Press, London 1985. Tells the story of a young girl uprooted from Jamaica for a loveless existence in England, who on her return to the Caribbean finds no sense of belonging there either. A very powerful and bleak novel which presents the psychological disorientation created by her alienation from both worlds. Joan Riley belongs to the same generation as Caryl Phillips. Her second novel *Waiting in the Twilight*, Women's Press, 1987, also deals with the plight of the woman whilst it tells of the struggle of one woman from the Caribbean to survive in an alien, racist, hostile environments in England. Joan Riley dedicates it to a whole generation of women from the Caribbean who took ship and sailed into the unknown to build a better future for their children.

Buchi Emecheta (Nigeria) *Second Class Citizen* and *In the Ditch* are largely autobiographical novels by the well known Nigerian writer. They tell of her extraordinary struggle to bring up her five children alone. In spite of racism, poverty and apalling living conditions she survives. Emecheta is concerned with experiences crucial to the black woman who constitutes the 'other' because of her gender as well as her colour.

Timothy Mo (Hong Kong), *Sour Sweet*, Abacus, London, 1983. The novel deals with the lives of the Chinese community in London and contrasts the violence of the Chinese 'mafia' in central London wiht the struggle of the Chen family for survival as owners of the Chinese take away restaurant, the Dah Ling. The novel won the Hawthorden Prize and was shortlisted for the Booker Prize.

POETRY

John Agard (Guyana), *Mangoes and Bullets*, Pluto Press, London, 1985. Selected and new poems by the winner of the Casa de las Americas prize, mostly in the nation language. This collection, from which 'Listen Mr. Oxford don' is taken, is both a hilarious defence of creole against the prejudices of academic English and a wonderful comic exposure of the philistine ignorance of the English, and their simplistic views of West Indian life.

David Dabydeen (Guyana), *Coolie Odyssy*, Dangaroo Press, 1988. The latest collection of poetry from the prize-winning poet.
The poems in this volume are taken from *Coolie Odyssy* .

Linton Kwesi Johnson (Jamaica), *Dread Beat and Blood* . Bogle L'Ouverture Publications, London, 1975. This is the most popular collection of poetry from the reggae poet who was a major force in establishing 'dub' poetry in Britain. He explores in particular the feelings of rage and violence which emerges under the pressure of racism.

Other volumes which deal with the themes of shattered illusions, racism, the schizophrenia caused by it and the rage and violence it creates include J.D. Douglas, *Caribbean Man's Blues*, Akira Press, London, 1985. Desmond Johnson, *Deadly Ending Season*, Akira Press, London, 1984; Martin Glynn, *De Ratchet A Talk*, Akira Press, London, 1985; and the anthology *News for Babylon*, Chalto and Windus, London, 1984, edited by James Berry.

Select Annotated Bibliography on Australian Multicultural Writing.

Rosa Capiello, *Oh Lucky Country*, University of Queensland Press, St. Lucia, 1981. (A raunchy and very funny account of a Neapolitan migrant woman's experiences in Sydney.)

Margaret Diesendorf, *Light*, Edwards & Shaw, Sydney, 1981. (Sensitive collection of poems which span Europe and Australia.)

Silvana Gardner, *Children of the Dragon*, Jacaranda Press, Queensland, 1985. (The most recent collection of poems by this fine painter and writer who comes from Dalmatia.)

Zeny Giles, *Between Two Worlds*, Phoenix Publications, Brisbane, 1984. (Collection of short stories which deal with cultural diversity in several settings.)

Amirah Inglis, *Amirah: An Un-Australian Childhood*, Heinemann, Victoria, 1983. (Witty and moving account of Russian Jews in Australia in the 1930s and 1940s.)

Antigone Kefala, *The Island*, Hale & Iremonger, Sydney, 1984. (Account of a young Greek woman's rite of passage into adulthood in New Zealand.)

Serge Liebermann, *A Universe of Clowns*, Phoenix Publications, Brisbane, 1983. (The second collection of short stories by this writer who captures the complexities of the Jewish experience in Australia.)

Uyen Loewald, *Child of Vietnam*, Hyland House, Victoria 1987. (First novel by the talented and politically committed Vietnamese writer.)

Angelo Loukakis, *Vernacular Dreams*, University of Queensland Press, St. Lucia, 1986. (The second collection of short stories by this Greek-Australian writer.)

David Martin, *Fox on My Door*, Collins Dove, Melbourne, 1987. (A fascinating autobiography by this prolific Hungarian-Jewish writer.)

George Papaellinos, *Ikons*, Penguin, Victoria, 1986. (Collection of short stories dealing with the experiences of second-generation Greek-Australians.)

P.O., *Ockers*, 1983. (The famous poem which presents a view of 'ockers' from Greek-Australian perspective. The king of the performance poets whose work should be snapped up whereever it is to be found.) Also recommended is his anthology, *Off the Record*, Penguin, Victoria, 1985.

Peter Skrzynecki, *Wild Dogs*, University of Queensland Press, 1987. (First collection of short stories by this Polish-Australian poet.)

Dimitris Tsaloumas, *The Observatory*, University of Queensland Press, St. Lucia, 1983. (The award winning collection of poems by the classical poet of Greek extraction.)

Ania Walwicz, *Writing*, Rigmarole Books, Melbourne, 1982. (Brilliant collection of prose poems by this performance artist of Polish-Jewish background.)

Judah Waten, *Alien Son*, Sun Books, Melbourne, 1952, 1978. (The classic collection of stories which remains one of the finest expressions of growing up Russian-Jewish in Australia.)

Some tools for teaching multicultural writing (compiled by Sneja Gunew, September 1987.)

Bibliographies:

Lolo Houbein, *Ethnic Writings in English from Australia*, Adelaide A.L.S. Working Papers, Department of English, University of Adelaide, 1984 (3rd revised and extended edition). (The pioneering compilation and deserving of a reprint.)

Peter Lumb and Anne Hazell (eds.), *Diversity and Diversion: an annotated bibliography of Australia Ethnic Minority Literature*, Hodja Educational Resources Co-operative Ltd., Richmond, Victoria, 1983. (excellent annotated guide for teachers.)

Anthologies:

Sneja Gunew (ed.), *Displacements: Migrant storytellers*, Deakin University Press, Victoria, 1982; and *Displacements II: Multicultural Storytellers*, Deakin University Press, 1987.

R.F. Holt (ed.), *The Strength of Tradition: Stories of the Immigrant Presence in Australia*, University of Queensland Press, St. Lucia, 1983.

M. Jurgensen (ed.), *Ethnic Australia*, Phoenix Publications, Brisbane, 1981.

P. Skrzynecki (ed.), *Joseph's Coat: an Anthology of Multicultural Writing*, Hale and Iremonger, New South Wales, 1985.

S. Gunew & J. Mahyuddin (eds.) *Beyond the Echo: Multicultural Women's Writing*, University of Queensland Press (forthcoming).

Journals:

Migrant 7, P.O. Box 2430V, GPO Melbourne 3001.

Outrider: a Journal of Multicultural Writing in Australia, P.O. Box 210, Indooroopilly, Queensland 4068.

Secondary Soources:

Jacques Delaruelle and Alexandra Karakostas-Seda (eds.) *Writing in Multicultural Australia 1984: an Overview,* Australia Council for the Literature Board, Sydney, 1985. (Proceedings of two conferences held in Sydney and Melbourne. Contains numerous papers with a variety of ethnic affiliations.)

Sneja Gunew, 'Discourses of Otherness: Migrants in Literature', *Prejudice in Print: the Treatment of Ethnic Minorities in Published works* . Proceedings of 'Prejudice in Print' Conference, edited by R. & H. Rasmussen, Melbourne Centre for Migrant Studies, Monash University, 1982, pp.48-58.
Sneja Gunew, 'Migrant women writers: who's on whose margins?', *Gender, Politics and Fiction,* ed. C. Ferrier, University of Queensland Press, St. Lucia, 1985, pp.163-178.
Sneja Gunew, 'Migrant Writing: Promising Territory', *Kunapipi,* 6.1, 1984, pp.12-19. (The above attempt to theorise ways of reading these ethnic texts, shows how current definitions of Australian literature will be changed by their inclusion.)

Jim Kable, '"the deep end of the schoolyard", or...Perspectives on the use of Australian literature with secondary E.S.L. students', *Topics in English as a Second Language,* 4, New South Wales Department of Education, 1983, pp.35-55.
Jim Kable, 'A multicultural perspective to Australian literature', *English Teachers Association (N.S.W.) Newsletter,* 5/83, pp.7-8.
Jim Kable, 'The immigrant experience: learning English and Australian literature ', *Australian Studies Bulletin,* 3 (April 1985), Deakin University, 1985, pp.21-24.
(The writer is an experienced teacher who has experimented with using ethnic writing in the classromm.)

Meryl Thompson, *Migrant as meaning-maker,* Curriculum Development Centre, Canberra, 1978. (Australian Studies in Language & Education Monograph Series.) (Explores how diverse cultural backgrounds and languages affect the process of creating meanings.)

Con Castan, *Conflicts of Love,* Phoenix Publications, Indooroopilly, 1986. (On the work of Vasso Kalamaris, the Greek poet and writer now living in Western Australia.)

L. Bodi & S. Jeffries (eds.) *The German Connection: Sesquicentenary Essays on German-Victorian Crosscurrents 1835-1985,* Monash University, 1985. (Collection of essays which deal with German-Australian cultural interactions.)

A.M. Nisbet & M. Blackman, *The French-Australian Connection,* University of New South Wales, 1984. (Papers from a symposium held on this topic.)

G. Rando (ed.) *Italian Writers in Australia: Essays and Texts,* University of Wollongong, 1983. (Fascinating collection of critical essays and writings by Italo-Australians.)

Vaccari Italian Historical Trust, *Italians in Australia* and *Australia's Italian Heritage,* Melbourne, 1987. (Proceedings of two conferences held in 1985 and 1986.)

Notes on Contributors.

Peter Nobel was born in Sweden in 1931, and practised law for over twenty years before he was appointed by the Swedish government in 1986 to be the first Ombudsman against Ethnic Discrimination in Sweden. He is a board member of the European Human Rights Foundation, a member of the international Institute of Humanitarian Law, and Research Consultant to the Scandinavian Institute of African Studies.

Salman Rushdie was born in Bombay in 1947 and now lives in London. His second novel, *Midnight's Children* was awarded the Booker Prize, The James Tait Memorial Prize, and the English Speaking Union Literary Award. His other publications include the novels *Grimus* and *Shame* which won the Prix du Meilleur Livre Etranger and a work of non-fiction, *The Jaguar Smile: A Nicaraguan Journey* . He is also the Author of *The New Empire: Racism in Britain* for Channel 4's 'Opinions' programme.

Claire Harris was born in Trinidad in 1937 and emigrated to Canada in 1966 after spending some time in Nigeria. In 1985 she was selected as the 'Best First Time Published Poet ' for the America's region in the Commonwealth Poetry Prize competition. Her books include *Fables from the Women's Quarters, Translation Into Fiction* and *Travelling to Find a Remedy* .

Caryl Phillips was born in St. Kitts, West Indies in 1955. In the same year his family moved to England. In 1979 he graduated from Oxford with a degree in English Literature. His first novel *The Final Passage* won the Malcom X Prize. This was followed by a second novel, *A State of Independence* . In 1987 his travel book, *The European Tribe* was published. The journey which it describes was written, Phillips said, 'as an attempt to come to terms with what it is like to feel both of, and not of, Europe.' He has also written pieces for stage, radio and television.

Aritha van Herk was born in Canada of Dutch parents in 1954. In 1978 she won the Seal Books $50,000 First Novel Award for *Judith* . Since then she has written two novels, *The Tent Peg*, which received much acclaim and has been translated into eight languages and *No Fixed Address* which was short-listed for the Canadian Governor General's Award. Dangaroo Press will publish a collection of her ficto/criticism *A Frozen Tongue* in 1989, a work which will examine Literary Speculations on Writing, Women and the West.

Antigone Kefala was born in Rumania of Greek parents. She spent her childhood there and at the end of the war moved with her family to Greece when after three years the family emigrated to New Zealand in 1951. After obtaining her M.A. degree from Victoria University, Wellington, she moved to Australia in 1959 where she has worked as an arts administrator. Her published works include two volumes of poetry, *The Alien* and *Thirsty Weather* and two novels, *The First Journey* and *The Island* .

Sue Kucharova was born in Czeckoslovakia in 1949. She left there in 1969 and after living for three years in England, USA and Canada working and learning English she arrived in Australia in 1973. In spite of the fact that she had no formal training in English she was accepted as a student at Macquarie University and obtained a degree in anthropology in 1977. She has done community-work and now works for the Australia Council. She started writing fiction in English in 1984 as a way to deal with her own ethnicity. She has a strong commitment to feminism and non-tokenistic multiculturalism.

Chitra Fernando was born in Sri Lanka. She now lectures in the School of English and Linguistics at Macquarie University, Sydney. Her stories have been published in Australia and Sri Lanka and her work is to be included in a new collection of migrant stories to be published in 1988.

Sneja Gunew was born in Germany in 1946 of a German mother and a Bulgarian father. She emigrated to Australia at the age of four and has worked as an academic in literature and women's studies since 1971. She recently edited a book on multicultural storytellers, *Displacements*, and is currently writing a book on multicultural writing in Australia.

Ania Walwicz was born in Poland in 1951 and came to Australia in 1963. For further information about her see her statement on p. 85.

Vilma Sirianni was born in Italy and came to Australia with her parents in 1954 when she was four. She writes both prose and poetry and is concerned with the tension between two cultures. She writes 'The choice between loyalty to one's family and duty to one's own future is not easy. The right choice was not made by many 'bi-cultural' children. The past still lives in us all. By writing down past episodes and remembered feelings I heal parts of me that still hurt. Many were wounded. My own writing has taught me that my parents too were amongst the wounded.'

Zeny Giles (Zenovia Doratis) was born in Sydney, Australia. Her father migrated from Cyprus, her mother from the island of Castellorize. In 1981 she won *The Age* Short Story Competition and her novel, *Between Two Worlds*, was published. Her play *The Bargain*, was workshopped at the 1984 National Playwrights Conference. Her collection of short stories about the hot bore baths at Moree is to be published by Penguin Books.

David Dabydeen was born in Guyana in 1954 and was sent to England in 1969 to join his father (see autobiographical statement pp.137-141). His first book of poems, *Slave Songs* was awarded the Commonwealth Poetry Prize and the

Cambridge University Quiller-Couch Prize. his second collection, *Coolie Odyssey* has just been published. It probes the experience of dispora, the journeying of peasant labourers from India to the Caribbean, then to Britain, dwelling on the dream of romances and the impotence of racial encounter. His other publications include *Hogarth's Blacks: Images of Blacks in Eighteenth Century Art* which won the £1,500 prize in the 1985 Greater London Literature Competition, *A Reader's Guide to West Indian and Black British Literature,* and *The Black Presence in English Literature.*

Peter Lyssiotis was born in Cyprus in 1949 and arrived in Australia in 1954. He is a photographer and photo-montage artist who combines image and text and has exhibited in various galleries. His work has appeared in numerous publications including *Meanjin, Arena, White Walls, Kunapipi* . Books published include *Journey of a Wise Electron* and *Three Cheers for Civilization.*

Sam Selvon was born in Trinidad in 1923 and in 1950 he emigrated to London where his first novel *A Brighter Sun* was published. In 1956 his novel *The Lonely Londoners* was published. This work has become a classic not only in West Indian Literature, but also in the literature of migration and exile. The novel deals with the mass migration of the West Indies to London in the 1950s, it's theme is the shattering of illusion and the reality of bondage. Beneath the comedy Selvon explores the psychology of deracination and rejection, the separation of self from body, the divorce of personality from flesh that racism effects.

Philip Salom was born in Western Australia in 1950. He has won the Commonwealth Poetry Prize on two occasions; in 1980 with *The Silent Piano and in 1987 with Sky Poems* . 'Migrants in the Sky' is from that volume.

Zia Moheddin was born in Pakistan and came to England in the early 50s. He was the first Asian to have his name in lights in the West End Theatre. His first appearance on the London stage was in 1960 where he played Dr. Aziz in *Passage to India,* a performance which was repeated on Broadway in 1962 for which he was nominated best actor by *Variety* . He returned to Pakistan in the 1970s where he was appointed Director General National Performing Ensemble. He left Pakistan after the military takeover in 1977. As well as appearing in films he has made numerous appearances on TV including leading parts in *Jewel in the Crown,* and *Mountbatten* . He currently produces and presents for Central Television the programme 'Here. Now'.

Kirsten Holst Petersen is a graduate of the University of Aarhus and the School of Oriental and African Studies, London University. She has lectured at universities in Denmark, Nigeria and Australia and for the past three years has been Danish Research Fellow at the Scandinavian Institute of African Studies, Uppsala, Sweden. She has published widely in the field of post-colonial studies in particular on African literature and has co-edited several volumes with Anna Rutherford, including *A Double Colonization: Colonial and Post Colonial Women's Writing* and *Cowries and Kobos: The West African Oral Tale and Short Story* . She is poetry editor of Dangaroo Press and the arts magazine, *Kunapipi* .

Nikos Kypraios was born on the Greek island of Samos. He studied in Athens and had his first exhibition there in 1968. He came to Australia in 1972. His work has been exhibited in Europe, Australia and America. Much of his work focusses on people's feelings, particularly on the feeling for people who live in the 'cold paranoic' environment of the big city.

Anna Rutherford is a graduate of the University of Newcastle, New South Wales, Australia. She has lectured at universities in Denmark, Nigeria and Australia, and is in charge of post-colonial studies at the University of Aarhus. She has published widely in the field of post-colonial studies, is director of Dangaroo Press and editor of *Kunapipi* . She is also on the editorial board of the *Journal of Commonwealth Literature, World Literature Written in English, Ariel,* and *Westerly,* and is international chairperson of the Association for Commonwealth Literature and Language Studies.

John Agard was born in Guyana and moved to England in 1977. He won the Cuban 'Casa de las Americas' poetry prize for his book, *Man to Pan* . A very popular performer on the poetry circuit he has referred to himself as a 'poetsonian' indicating his kinship with the satirical spirit of the Calypsonian. He is also a very successful author of children's books and his latest book *Lend Me Your Wings* was shortlisted for the Smarties Prize.

Back issues of the DOLPHIN still available:

No. 6 (November 1982): Culture & Narcissism. The Significance of Christopher Lasch.

No. 7 (May 1983): Pigebørn og Kvindemennesker. Kvindelitteratur, kvindesituation og feministiske perspektiver i England og USA.

No. 8 (October 1983): Joyce Centenary Offshoots. James Joyce 1882-1982.

No. 9 (April 1984): Coyote Was Here. Essays on Contemporary Native American Literary and Political Mobilization.

No. 10 (October 1984): George Orwell and 1984, six essays.

No. 11 (April 1985): Inventing the Future. Science Fiction in the Context of Cultural History and Literary Theory.

No. 13 (April 1986): Communicative Competence in Foreign Language Learning and Teaching.

No. 14 (December 1986): British Drama in the Eighties. Texts and Contexts.

Forthcoming:

No. 16 (Summer 1988): Something to Believe in. Writer Responses to the Spanish Civil War.

No. 17 (Autumn 1988): Popular Fictions.